THE STORY

OF

INDIA

THE STORY
OF
INDIA.

BY

DEMETRIUS C. BOULGER.

GYAN

Published by

GYAN

Gyan Publishing House
5, Ansari Road
Daryaganj, New Delhi-110002
Phone: 011-47034999, 9811692060
E-mail: books@gyanbooks.com

Distribution Network
gyanbooks.com
India, USA, Canada, UK, Australia

ISBN: 978-93-6208-550-4 (PB)
First Published, 1897

2nd Impression 2024

Printed at: Gyan Press, Delhi.

THE STORY OF INDIA
Author: DEMETRIUS C. BOULGER

THE STORY OF THE EMPIRE.

Edited by Howard Angus Kennedy.

THE STORY
OF
INDIA.

BY

DEMETRIUS C. BOULGER.

London:
HORACE MARSHALL & SON.
Temple House,
E.C.

CONTENTS.

INDIA AND HER PEOPLE.

THE story of India is that of a land quite different from any other in the British Empire. Its population of three hundred millions is immensely larger than any that a European power has undertaken to rule elsewhere, and it confronts us with problems more stubborn than any we have to solve in America, Australasia, or even Africa. It cannot compete with Canada or Australia in actual size of territory; still, it is thirty times as large as England, and larger than the continent of Europe without Russia. Its general outline on the map is familiar enough, a great triangle pointing southward into the Indian Ocean, and northward a huge dome-shaped mass rising high into Central Asia. Every variety of climate is to be found in India; for her million and a half of square miles include every height of land, from the level of the sea to the tallest mountain peaks on the surface of the globe. There is plenty of variety among the people, too. Those of the north-west and centre have a strain of Aryan blood and are more or less closely akin to ourselves; those of the north-east and Burmah are more like the Chinese; and those of the south belong to the Dravidian branch of the human family. The peoples of India vary in creed, language, and civilisation as they do in race. The Hindus, divided into innumerable sects and worshipping more gods than there are inhabitants; the Mahomedans, with their one god and a prophet; the Jains, Buddhists, Sikhs and Devil-worshippers,—differ from each other not only in their faith but in their history, manners and dress. They differ, indeed, far more widely than do the inhabitants of Protestant and Roman Catholic Europe. The principal languages in use are descended from the Sanskrit (as the French, Spanish and Italian are all derived from Latin), or belong to a separate group called the Dravidian; but it is reckoned that over 300 languages and dialects are spoken in India. Then it is a mistake to suppose that the inhabitants are all on the same intellectual level, for some are mere barbarians and others are full of elaborate and curious learning. Finally, the social distinctions which mock our professions of democratic equality at home exist in a peculiarly aggravated form in India, where the high-caste Brahmin reckons his food polluted if the very shadow of a low-caste Sudra or an out-caste Pariah falls upon it.

In only one way are the people of India united, and that is—in being the people of India. In the far past, which most of them know nothing of, some of their ancestors came from distant lands; but now they are all at home. The white men who rule them, on the other hand, are foreigners, who come and govern and go away in an endless succession of arrivals and departures. The white man could never be at home in India, even if the natives adopted his customs and his creed. I have spoken of mountains; but these cover a comparatively small part of the country. The India where the millions live and where the governing has to be done is a hot and feverish land. Here the white man may live for a time and keep his faculties fresh enough for adminis trative work, with frequent visits to the healthier hill-country and a trip to England every few years. By the greatest care in eating and drinking, by adapting himself to the necessities of the climate as the unbending Englishman finds it hard to do, and by the help of quinine, he may even ward off malaria and cholera for many years; but the climate has its effect at last, either on the man himself or on his descendants. Few white men even attempt to bring up their children in India; and it is said that in those few cases their descendants never survive to the fourth generation.

There are two other ways in which a large majority of the natives, though not all, are unhappily united. They are poor, and they are ignorant. Their poverty is not that of people who make themselves miserable by always wanting something they cannot afford. It is the poverty of those who have just enough to keep body and soul together when all is going well. When the crops fail they must simply lie down and die of starvation unless their masters, the Government and the charitable British public, hasten to feed them. As for what we call education, or even the smattering of knowledge that we give in our elementary schools, not one native in twenty has yet received it. The other nineteen have what is worse than the mere absence of knowledge—they have superstition in the most burdensome quantities. Their lives are governed and hampered in many directions by ridiculous beliefs, their minds oppressed and disturbed by appalling suspicions. For instance—when the local authorities order a new bridge to be built, there is a common and firmly-fixed idea among the villagers that the white men kidnap native children and bury them under the foundations. The taking of a census gives rise to a belief that the Government is searching for a miraculous child, with milk instead of blood in his veins, who will overthrow British rule—as Herod sought for the infant Christ. Small-pox is cured, the ignorant natives think, by taking the "crusts" formed by the disease and exposing them at the cross-roads; and cholera is supposed to be carried from village to village by a scapegoat. In some parts of the country every family boasts of a witch; and men commit suicide in order that their ghosts may avenge imaginary wrongs.

What is to be the future of these people, and what part are we to take in that future? These are the great questions the British public will have to answer. Fortunately for us, the life of the East moves slowly, and we are not driven to solve the problem in a day; but a traveller does not wait till his journey is half done before asking himself where he is going.

Split up as they are by the barriers of blood, of sect, of social custom, and of distance, it is hard to imagine the peoples of India welded into a nation till centuries have gone by. To suggest that the natives of India should now be left to govern themselves would show an ignorance equal to their own. We might as well dress them in tall hats and trousers and expect them to be comfortable as equip them with a Parliamentary Franchise and expect them to show the political energy and intelligence of a self-governing nation. Nevertheless, the people of India are not going to remain sunk in ignorance for ever. They are able to learn, and they will learn. When they have won knowledge, when education has developed their capacity and at the same time made them more like one another, they will certainly not rest content as subjects of a foreign Power. They will claim the place of citizens, and they will get it. Meanwhile, in the long period which must elapse before such a claim can possibly be justified or enforced, the ruling power itself may be greatly altered. If the British Empire is then in existence, it will probably be stronger than it is now; but its strength will not be that of a little and populous kingdom controlling vast outlying territories with small or uncivilised populations all over the world—it will be the strength of a great alliance or federation of strong and self-governing nations. Will there be no room in such an elastic system for a nation which, though not of British blood, has had the British Empire for her foster-mother? May we not venture to hope that when India has the choosing of her own future she will connect herself with the nation to which she is now involuntarily bound?

There are other forces than gratitude—which, indeed, is said to have no existence in politics; and it is not always kindest to do what would make others most grateful to us at the moment. But it is our plain duty not to do anything in India for which history will say that India was justly ungrateful. We were not thinking of India's interests when we took possession of her, and even now there are some who would have us treat her as if she existed chiefly for our benefit. From this point of view, we are to feel a miserly satisfaction that India furnishes careers and salaries for a multitude of English officials. We are to thank heaven that the frontier tribes are wicked enough to give our armies practice in the art of fighting. We are to manipulate Indian tariffs so as to prevent the Indian manufacturer from competing with us in his own country. Happily our responsible statesmen have committed themselves to a principle in direct opposition to all this—the principle that in our government of India the interests of India must be considered first. It is our business now to see that this admirable policy is carried out, and carried out with boldness and with insight. If we are to care for Indian interests we must make it our business to develop the capacities of her people as we develop the capacities of our own. We must not be frightened out of our policy of education because a handful of the natives whom we have educated use their new-found power to diminish our own: on the other hand, we must not be afraid of putting down these educated gentlemen with a firm hand when they take unfair advantage of their fellow-countrymen's ignorance and try to upset our rule with lies. We have rightly admitted natives to a share in the government of India; but we must not imagine that those natives who can most easily pass an examination of the English fashion are the best qualified to rule their fellow-countrymen. We must not be checked in our education of the people by a fear lest when they are educated we shall not be able to govern them,—any more than we should allow them to cut each other's throats because the population is growing too dense, or let the plague desolate their cities because they are prejudiced against sanitation.

India is valuable to the British Empire because it forms a station on the imperial highway between east and west. It is an important link in the chain of islands and territories from which our armies and navies can dart out upon any part of the world at short notice. This would not justify us in keeping India if she were a State with a moderately developed national existence. As things are, by leaving India we should not only give up an advantage to ourselves but should be doing the worst injury in our power to India, for Russia would at once step into our place, and would make short work of any rudiments of British liberty we had introduced.

That we have begun to endow India with the most valuable gifts we have ourselves received, there is no doubt whatever. We have given her peace and order. We have given her an example of religious toleration, which she greatly needs, by officially respecting her forms of religion except when they degenerate into murder and suicide. At the same time we have unofficially put Christianity within her reach, with its practical ideals of truth, honesty, and disinterested humanity. We have given her a firm and pure administration of justice by officials who, if they are foreign, are at least impartial and incorruptible. We have set over them a government which, as they are beginning to understand, has some genuine concern for the welfare of the people governed. We must continue in this path, vigorously upholding the dignity of our position as ruler and arbiter among the peoples of India, but making the welfare of those peoples and the development of their highest faculties the principal object of our rule. Only on these terms can the British democracy consent to play the autocrat of India.

A few facts drawn from government sources had better be given here for the benefit of readers who want more precise information on some of the points mentioned above. The blue-book quoted is the "Statistical Abstract relating to British India"; and the issue of that publication gives figures for the official year 1894-95.

The population of British India—that is, of the territories under direct British government—was 198,860,606 in 1881 and had increased to 221,172,952 when the last census was taken in 1891. The population of the states which are governed by native rulers under the eye of British representatives increased in those ten years from 54,932,908 to 66,050,479. The figures for 1891 show that of the total population 146,727,296 were males, and only 140,496,135 were females. British India covers 964,993 square miles and Native States 595,167; but in the former the average number of persons living on every square mile is 229 and in the native states it is only 111. The highest average is 471 per square mile in Bengal, and the next is 436 in the North West Provinces and Oude; while the lowest average in British India is 35 in Upper Burmah—the native state of Cashmere falling still lower to 31 per square mile. In England we had in the same year 540 people to the square mile, and in Scotland 134. The next census in 1901 will doubtless show that India's population continues to rapidly increase. The great famine of 1897 has not been allowed to have the fatal results of previous times of scarcity; and the plague, though terribly fatal where it raged, was kept within a comparatively small space.

As to the general death rate, figures collected with reference to 217,941,325 of the population show that 33 in every thousand died in 1894 95. The actual number of deaths was 7,301,170, of which 4,987,304 were caused by fevers, 521,975 by cholera, 261,996 by dysentery and diarrhœa, 43,623 by small-pox, and 93,110 by injuries. That was a particularly unhealthy year, worse even than the bad year 1892-93. In 1893-94 the death rate was only 25. Wild beasts destroyed as many as 24,431 lives in the twelve months of 1894-95, and 21,583 of these deaths were caused by snakes. Tigers killed 864 persons, leopards 371, wolves 227, bears 111 and elephants 68, while 1,226 human beings were slain by jackals, alligators, wild pigs, scorpions, and other animals. The number of cattle killed in the same way was 97,371, of whom tigers took more than a third. In the same year the Government paid about £6,700 in rewards for the destruction of 102,210 snakes, 1,311 tigers, 4,052 leopards, 1,456 bears, 2,614 wolves, 935 hyenas, 28 elephants and 3,051 other beasts.

During the year the loss of population by

emigration was only 17,932, of whom 11,173 went to the West Indies, 1,964 to South Africa, 1,082 to Fiji, 486 to Mauritius, and 1,219 to Dutch Guiana.

Of the whole population (287,223,431) as many as 171,735,390 are living by agriculture, 3,645,849 by the provision and care of cattle, and 25,468,017 by earthwork and general labour. Manufactures provide a living for 29,482,731; while 5,600,153 are in the employ of the State or local bodies (besides 664,422 in the army and navy), and 5,672,191 belong to the learned and artistic professions. Those who are rich enough to live without working number 4,773,993; and 1,562,981 others are described as having "undefined and disreputable means of livelihood." On the last date mentioned 96,564 persons were in prison.

There are 126,244 lepers in India, 458,868 blind, and 196,761 deaf-mutes; while 74,289 are officially reported as insane.

The educational returns show 2,997,558 males and 197,662 females under instruction. Of the rest of the population only 11,554,035 males and 543,495 females can even read and write.

The people of British India, of course including the Europeans, received only 403,525,902 letters, newspapers and other packets through the post during the year—

about one seventh of the number handled by the post office in the United Kingdom for a population of less than 40,000,000.

The census of religions shows this result:—Hindus, 207,731,727; Mahomedans, 57,321,164; Aboriginals, 9,280,467; Buddhists, 7,131,361; Christians, 2,284,380; Sikhs, 1,907,833; Jains, 1,416,638; Parsees, 89,904; Jews, 17,194; and 42,763 "others."

The Christian population includes 247,790 persons wholly or partly of European blood, and of these 130,988 belong to the Church of England. The native Christians, numbering 2,036,590, are divided thus:—Roman Catholics, 1,243,529; Syrians, 200,449; Baptists, 186,487; Church of England, 164,028; Lutherans, 64,243; Presbyterians, 30,915; and 146,939 of other denominations. The Nestorians are believed—we have done with the Blue Book now—to have first planted Christianity in India, in the third century. In the fourteenth century the Roman Catholics began to arrive; and in 1706 a German Protestant Mission was begun under Danish protection. In the summer of 1793 England sent out William Carey to begin the great missionary movement now carried on by a number of British and American societies, who work as a rule harmoniously and without overlapping and competition. This is no place for a discussion of missionary methods. It is enough to say on the one hand that the natives returned as Christians have imbibed the spirit of Christianity in varying degrees and, on the other hand, that missionary work has largely Christianised the spirit and opinions of very many who do not call themselves Christians. From whatever point of view the aims and methods of this movement are regarded, there has been and still is in the men who carry it on enough earnestness, self-sacrifice, and intelligence to compel our admiration.

HOWARD ANGUS KENNEDY.

August 20th, 1897.

CHAPTER I.

INDIA BEFORE OUR TIME.

WHEN in 1579 Thomas Stephens, the first Englishman to visit India, resided at Salsette, an island now forming part of the proud City of Bombay, the Mogul dynasty in the person of the wise and illustrious Akbar had established itself on the throne of Delhi, and a settled and successful Government existed throughout the northern and more important portion of the peninsula of Hindustan. When Captain Hawkins and Sir Thomas Roe appeared in 1608 and 1616 respectively at Agra and Ajmere in the character of Ambassadors from James the First, the Mogul dynasty had attained the zenith of its power under Shah Jehangir. Those Englishmen found India a practically united Empire with a magnificent Court and obedient to the sway of a Potentate whose wealth and military power made him appear more than the equal of the rulers of

Europe. The visitors could not be expected to know that what they saw was not the normal position of the country, or to realise that they had only chanced to arrive at the moment of the triumph of one of those invaders of India who in two thousand years have made it their favourite battle ground and prey, from the time of Alexander to that of Nadir Shah and his successor, the Afghan, Ahmed Shah.

It is desirable to make it clear beyond all possibility of misconception that India before our time was not a single united State. Even the Mogul dynasty, the most successful of all alien dominations in the Peninsula until we came on the scene, never subdued the whole country; its authority in the first century of its existence was either successfully defied or speedily cast off by the Rajputs and Marathas, and it would have been overthrown by the militant chiefs of Hinduism before the French and English fought for supremacy in the Deccan but for the terrible inroads of Nadir and Ahmed uniting the discordant and hostile elements of Indian society to meet a great and common danger. The normal condition of India was marked by disunion, internecine strife and inability to resist a bold and active invader. There is no case on record of the races of Hindustan having successfully repelled an invader from the North West,—that is to say one coming through or from Afghanistan. The Mogul conquerors themselves had come from that quarter in the time of Akbar's grandfather Baber; and their conquest—considering the smallness of their force, for Baber had less than 5,000 men with which to emulate the deeds of his ancestors Tamerlane and Genghis by the subjection of India—was one of the most remarkable in the whole list. But even the Mogul conquerors in turn had to succumb whenever the Persian and Afghan conquerors advanced their standards to the historic plain of Paniput.

The evidence of the disunion of India was clear even in the time of Alexander the Great. It was over kings who would not combine that he triumphed between the Indus and the Beas; and when the chivalry of heroic India was hastening to continue the struggle, the tame submission and subsequent co-operation of Porus ensured the safe and unmolested retreat of the Greek army. India was not called upon to face the ordeal of another foreign invasion for nearly a thousand years after Alexander; but compensation was found for this tranquillity in an increased amount of internal strife. The petty Hindu kings warred on each other with little intermission. Not one of them was strong enough to gain any wide or durable ascendancy; even the much-vaunted kingdom of

Kanauj controlled a region smaller than the present Punjab, and the great majority of the Rajput kinglets esteemed themselves fortunate if they could retain their own hereditary territories. The India of that day may not have been as miserable as this ceaseless struggle might lead one to think, for the wars were conducted by a code of chivalry which deprived them of a sanguinary character. The motives of the contestants were not ambition or a settled design of conquest, but racial pride and the traditional claim of one House to rank before another. But if civil strife did not make India as poor or as unhappy as would have been the result if conducted on the sterner lines of our Western methods, it unquestionably made her weak and insecure against foreign aggression. Her weakness was increased because for centuries no external aggressor presented himself, and the spirit of patriotism was never called forth to quell the prevalent disunion.

When the peril came it appeared in an unexpected manner and was attended by a circumstance which eventually added another and most potent cause to the many already existing elements of strife and disunion in India. In the seventh century of our era the Arab emirs who began the propagation of Mahomedanism by the subjection of Perias turned aside from their threatened movement westwards to march on India. It is said that their anger had been provoked by the seizure of one of their trading ships on the coast of Guzerat. If so, the act of some petty chief involved the whole state in many misfortunes which were not limited to the period of the Arab incursions. In fact, the importance of the Arab invasions is not so much what they accomplished themselves as it is that they marked the commencement of Mahomedan inroads which continued in one form or other for the better part of a thousand years.

In the seventh century the Arabs overran the countries which are now called Scinde and Afghanistan. During the following century they made good their positions in those territories, but failed to make any further headway, repulsed on the one side by the chivalry of the Rajputs and checked on the other by the snows of the Hindu Kush mountains. In the ninth century they lost Scinde, but by that time Mahomedanism formed a solid wedge in Western Asia from the Aral sea to the Indian Ocean. It had however not crossed the river Indus, where it was opposed by as firm a front on the part of Hindu Brahminism as on the west by the Christian churches. Having lost the only Indian province they conquered, the Arab attempts against the peninsula may be regarded as concluded, but their colonies, in conjunction with native chiefs who had embraced Mahomedanism, firmly held the whole of Afghanistan, and at least two dynasties which became historically famous originated with them. It is with these rather than with the Arabs that the first Mahomedan invasions of India must be connected.

At Ghuzni, famous as a fortress to the present day, the more powerful of these dynasties had established itself. Of necessity there were relations between it and the princes of India, and causes of strife soon arose. It must in fairness be recorded that on this occasion the Hindus were the aggressors. Filled with pride and self-confidence, they forced the mountain passes and marched on Ghuzni. They were signally defeated by Sebukhtegin, the ruler of Ghuzni, who also skilfully cut oft their line of retreat, and thus compelled them to purchase a safe exit from Afghanistan at a price which will stand for a million pounds. On their return to India the question was debated in solemn council whether the indemnity should be paid, the Brahmins arguing that there was no need now to pay the money, while the Rajput warriors pleaded for the due fulfilment of the promise. The King was weak and yielded to the civil councillors, but the price paid for this breach of honour was immense.

Sebukhtegin seized Peshawur and the passages of the Indus. Then he died; but he left to his son and successor, Mahmud, the legacy of exacting retribution from the false Hindus. Well was that task fulfilled! In 25 years Mahmud of Ghuzni led sixteen victorious invading armies into India, his two most signal successes being marked by the overthrow of the Kingdom of Kanauj and the plunder of the holy city and shrine of Somnath. The Punjab, wrested by him from the Rajputs, now became the base of Mahomedan enterprise and encroachment within the recognised geographical limits of Hindustan.

The Ghuzni dynasty existed for 150 years after the death of Mahmud, and when it succumbed it was not to any Hindu opponent. A rival Mahomedan family and race in Western Afghanistan, known as the Ghor dynasty, took upon itself the task which had become too heavy for Mahmud's degenerate successors. About the year 1190 Mahomed of Ghor seized Ghuzni and occupied the Punjab. He followed up these preliminary measures in the orthodox manner by plundering Delhi in 1193 and sacking Kanauj in the following year. He might have equalled the total of the Ghuzni conqueror's invasions if three Rajput warriors, animated by patriotism, had not murdered him in his tent during the night.

The Hindus could not offer a combined and warlike resistance to an assailant inferior both in numbers and resources, but they could produce heroes capable of isolated feats of daring.

The generals who had fought under the Ghor conqueror became Indian chiefs and kings. His most successful lieutenant founded the dynasty of the slave kings, and from that time onward the Punjab and the whole of north-west India was subject to Mahomedan rule. The first break in this rule was when the Sikh chief Runjeet Singh shook off the Afghan yoke at the beginning of the present century. Even the incursions of the formidable Mongols made no alteration in this respect. In the time of the dreaded Genghis, first of "the scourges of God," they merely brushed past the border regions of India on their return from Persia to Mongolia. They found North-West India Mahomedan, and their devastating legions, as they retired satiated with slaughter and laden with plunder under Tamerlane—the conqueror who feasted for five days in Delhi while his soldiers butchered the inhabitants so that the dead were piled high in the streets of that capital—left it unaffected in its constitution and only smitten by an appalling calamity. When the Mongols returned for the third and last time in the person of Baber at the beginning of the 16th century, they had themselves become Mahomedans and were consequently of the same creed as the Afghan Lodis reigning at Delhi whom they overthrew.

Unlike his predecessors Genghis and Tamerlane, Baber the Lion was not the leader of a host of marauders, but a great statesman aiming at clear and definite results. With far smaller resources than his ancestors he achieved more splendid and more durable results. Baber, who made his capital at Cabul in preference to either Delhi or Lahore, did not long enjoy the supremacy he established throughout the Punjab and the adjacent Provinces. He founded the Mogul dynasty in 1526, and four years later he died leaving a divided inheritance. His elder son Humayoun became Emperor of India, with his capital at Delhi; his younger son Kamran, the abler and more ambitious of the two, got the Afghan provinces and established his seat of power at Cabul. A struggle for empire ensued between these brothers, but although Humayoun retained the style of Emperor for 26 years, he was a fugitive in Persia during the latter part of them, and Kamran remained victorious until the genius of Humayoun's son Akbar turned the scale against him.

Akbar was the true founder of the Mogul dynasty. In 49 years, from 1556 to 1605, this great contemporary of Queen Elizabeth assured by the astuteness of his policy not less than by the terror of his arms the Mogul conquest of India, and extended his authority to Goa on the one side and the mouths of the Ganges on the other. The system on which Akbar acted was a new one. He determined to win over to his person and cause the noblest race of India and to associate them in his work. However contemptible were the efforts of the oldest Aryan races of India to hold their own against the North-Western invaders, the Rajputs, who have been not incorrectly termed the Normans of India, preserved throughout these national misfortunes an unblemished reputation for personal courage and chivalry. Akbar made it his first object to win over some at least of the chief representatives of this noble people to his side, and he succeeded in the case of the great and still illustrious family of Jeypore. He married a Princess of that House, and her brother, Raja Man Singh, became the generalissimo of his armies. His exploits cannot be recited here, but he was perhaps the greatest military leader whom the soil of India ever produced. Akbar took his statesmen as well as his soldiers from the Hindus. The name of Todar Mall is still among the greatest in India as a financier and law-giver, while that of Abu Fazl remains unequalled among the wise and courageous counsellors whom a despot is fortunate to find at his elbow.

The edifice erected by Akbar was as firmly planted as ever in the reign of his son and successor Jehangir when the English envoy Sir Thomas Roe came, hat in hand as it were, to beg favours from "the Mightie Emperour commonly knowne as the Great Mogul." No one could have foreseen that before another generation passed away the Moguls would be humiliated in the field by the Persians under Shah Abbas, and threatened by a Hindu uprising in the formation of the Maratha League under the redoubtable Sivaji. Sir Thomas Roe could not be expected to show a prophetic instinct. His instructions were very simple. He was to get a "factory" or trading agency at Surat and to "procure such rarities as China and Japan afforded." As he accomplished the former portion of his task—mainly it is said through the celebrated Nur Mahal, the Queen of Jehangir—his embassy must be termed successful; but in one sense it was misleading, for it strengthened the view that India was a vast united Empire of immense power and resources far beyond the reach of our greatest efforts, and that the utmost we could expect were such crumbs from the Imperial table as the mighty Emperor might condescend to cast us. It was this belief that led our early adventurers to look to the isles of the Eastern Archipelago rather than to India itself for trade, and that paralysed the hand of the East India Company in its dealings with the Native Powers until Clive indicated a broader and more successful course. The characteristics of India before our time were disunion and inability to use its immense latent strength for defensive purposes. At the moment we came into contact with India there happened to be established what seemed an imposing and powerful Government. It was an episode, not a solid and durable creation. The swing of the pendulum soon carried Mogul India back to its natural condition of disunion which placed it at the mercy of aggressors whether they came through the passes or across the seas.

CHAPTER II.

OUR MERCHANT ADVENTURERS.

THE discovery of America by Columbus in 1492 and the rounding of the Cape of Good Hope by Vasco da Gama in 1497 were the two events that turned the energy of the maritime races of Europe in the direction of India. Both were enterprises undertaken for the quest of the Indies. While the Portuguese were actively establishing their position and extending their trade by the south-east route, the northern nations and especially England clung to the hope that the North-west Passage might still prove the highway to the markets of the East. Henry the Seventh gave John Cabot his royal authority to discover that passage in 1496, before da Gama had sailed from Lisbon. Sebastian Cabot renewed his father's attempt at half a century's interval; Sir Hugh Willoughby went to his death on the same errand; Martin Frobisher, John Davis and others followed on their track; and the sixteenth century closed with English maritime enterprise baffled in its most attractive outlet by the icepack and frozen seas beyond Baffin's Bay. During that century the Portuguese claimed a monopoly of trade and navigation east of the Cape, and they kept it until the Dutch entered the field as competitors in 1595 and were followed a few years later by the English.

Undoubtedly the repeated defeats in the quest of a North-west passage led English mariners to attempt to reach the Indies by a different route. When Sir Francis Drake left our shores in 1577 to sail round the globe it was deemed that the Portuguese held the Cape route too securely to make it safe for Englishmen to go that way; Drake therefore sailed westwards and rounded Cape Horn. The success of his cruise was immense, and is not to be depreciated by the fact that he never reached India or touched at any land except one of the Molucca isles. Drake's example was followed by Thomas Cavendish, who may be called the first English navigator of the China seas, as he reached the Ladrones, not far from Hong Kong and Macao, in 1587. It was the voyages of Drake and Cavendish that led the Spanish King to complain that those navigators had infringed the divine rights of Spain, which then included

Portugal, by sailing round the world; Queen Elizabeth made the proud retort that what the Spaniards did it was lawful for the English to do also, since the sea and air were common to all men. That diplomatic passage of arms was followed by the Invincible Armada; and the overthrow of the Spanish fleet, besides saving England from invasion, opened to her the barred doors of the Indies. If the naval supremacy of Spain had not been shattered on that occasion it may be doubted whether the fitful efforts of a few Drakes and Cavendishes would ever have resulted in our holding "the Golden East in fee." It was not merely that the successes of that running seafight from Eddystone to Berwick Head gave our sailors and captains confidence in their superiority over the Dons, but around our shores lay the wrecks of the very guard-ships that deterred the boldest of our countrymen from using the Portuguese high road past St. Helena and the Cape.

The obstacles in the path of Englishmen using the direct route being removed, it only remained to turn to the best account the new avenue of trade with the Indies. The first attempts made by Englishmen to reach India were disastrous. Several ships were lost; and to add to the mortification of the London merchants the Dutch under Houtman established themselves in Java before the last year of the sixteenth century, while England, who had shattered Spain's naval power, had not yet been able to fly the St. George's Cross on the Indian Ocean.

These were weighty reasons closely touching our national pride. For a hundred years and more we had been looking for a way to the Indies. Heroes whose names are forgotten or rarely mentioned had given their lives for the cause. A magnificent national triumph had consolidated our own position, raised the enthusiasm of the people and the confidence of the Government, and finally removed the Cerberus who watched the gate to the Indies. These were the causes which led our merchant adventurers eastwards. It was the knowledge that our mariners had realized Elizabeth's assertion that the sea was common to all, that banded the wealthy citizens of London in an undertaking which was adventurous, which should be profitable, but which above all was the natural consummation of a national purpose followed under every discouragement during four reigns. It is magnifying a petty incident to say, as has been said, that our trade with the Indies began because the Dutch in 1599 raised the price of pepper from three shillings to more than double that sum a pound. If there had been no increase in the price of pepper the disastrous attempts made in 1591 and again in

1596 to reach India would still have had successors, and there would still have been "a company of merchants of London trading to the East Indies."

The association which bore that name was incorporated by Royal Charter on the last day of the year 1600. Elizabeth took a special interest in promoting its fortunes, even sending an ambassador overland to the Court of the Great Mogul, which however he did not reach. Having obtained the charter, the merchants and others—chiefly members of the official nobility—subscribed the money to fit out the ships for a voyage and to entitle them to a share in the profits. The first of these voyages began early in 1601, when five ships —the "Mare Scourge," or "Scourge of the Sea" (subsequently named "Red Dragon"), the "Hector," the "Ascension," the "Guest" (or more probably the "Gift"), and the "Susan"—under command of Captain James Lancaster, sailed from the Thames. This expedition was fairly successful in a commercial respect, and resulted in the opening of direct trade with Java, where a station or "House of Trade" was established at Bantam. On the return of Sir James Lancaster, who was knighted for the voyage, Elizabeth was dead and James the 1st was king; but the new monarch took as much interest in trade with the Indies as his great predecessor. A second voyage was therefore arranged for in the same year as Lancaster's return, and four of his vessels composed the expedition, for it seems probable that the "Dragon" was identical with the "Red Dragon" or "Mare Scourge." This voyage was under the command of Sir Henry Middleton. Up to the year 1612 twelve of these voyages may be counted, and with one exception they were all successful, paying the "adventurers" from 100 to 200 per cent., and making the English flag known from the Persian Gulf to the seas of Siam, Tonquin, and Japan. Captain Hawkins, who was attached to the third of these voyages, proceeded to Agra, the favourite residence of the Mogul Emperor, and resided there for three years as envoy from King James. While the bulk of the commerce now established was with the Eastern Archipelago, and with Japan, where Captain Saris founded the factory of Firando in 1613, the English succeeded in carrying on some trade through Surat, a town on the Taptee where the Portuguese had an important station, but as the new-comers had no licence from the Great Mogul to establish a factory at that town they were not on an equality with the Portuguese. Hawkins had been sent to Agra to get that licence, but although civilly entertained he did not succeed, and it was not until Sir Thomas Roe arrived as ambassador that his request was complied with. In the meantime much had happened that indirectly promoted the attainment of the object the English adventurers had in their hearts.

The Portuguese, firmly established at Surat, resented the appearance of the English near the chief place of trade in India, and resorted to force with a view of repelling the English, or at the least of discrediting and humiliating them in the eyes of the natives. For several years fights between the English and their rivals went on at the mouth of the Taptee and in the gulf of Cambay. Sir Henry Middleton, commander of the sixth voyage, fought a stiff fight with the Portuguese in 1611 before he could land at Cambay. A more serious encounter was fought in the following year, when the "Dragon" and "Osiander" under Captain Thomas Best were opposed at Swalley by 16 Portuguese vessels and a large number of small boats. Desultory fighting between them continued for three months, during which period Best was constantly pressing the Mogul Governor for authority to establish a factory at Surat; but when his pertinacity was rewarded with the necessary charter he took umbrage because it was sent as a private letter, refused to receive it, and sailed away in the beginning of 1613. The credit of obtaining the Surat factory and of establishing the martial credit of the English people has been given to Best; whereas the main result was due to his successor, the gallant Downton. It was Downton who led the first of the "Joint Stock Voyages," in which the enormous sum (for that day) of £1,600,000 was invested by 954 persons.

No English ship appeared off Swalley in 1613, but late in the following year a flotilla of 4 ships under Captain Downton arrived. The vessels were the "New Year's Gift," the "Hector," the "Hope" and the "Solomon," and they seem to have presented a superior fighting force to previous squadrons. No sooner was the arrival of the English ships known than the Portuguese Admiral at Goa fitted out a large expedition to attack them; but, whether through the greater skill and courage of the English sailors or because the Portuguese were over-confident, this superior force was decisively defeated with a loss of 350 Portuguese soldiers and sailors. This was the victory that established the reputation of the English, and that simplified the task of Sir Thomas Roe. The right to establish a factory at Surat, with minor or dependent factories at Gogra, Cambay and Ahmedabad, was really won at the sword's point from the Portuguese in Swalley roads. Having gained this triumph Downton continued his cruise to Bantam in Java, where he died suddenly, "lamented, admired, unequalled." The epitaph was uttered over him that he was "the true hero, piety and valour being seasoned by gravity and modesty." Among the early promoters of our trade in the East Downton, the long forgotten, whose laurels were transferred to Best, deserves a prominent and honourable place.

The majesty and power of the Great Mogul somewhat appalled our merchant adventurers, and led them the more willingly perhaps to follow in the wake of the Dutch, who had made the Archipelago the seat of their Eastern trade. There were the spice islands, and for a long time spices represented the staple product of the East in the eyes of Europeans. The chief inducement to proceed there was the absence of any powerful or arrogant potentate at whose mercy foreign traders held their lives and their property. But if the English representatives experienced opposition at the hands of the Portuguese at Swalley and along the western coast of India, it was small compared with that they met with from the more energetic and determined Dutchmen when they intruded on Java, Sumatra and the Moluccas. For six or seven years the struggle was carried on with a bitterness and ferocity on the Dutch side unexampled in the long competition for commercial supremacy in the East; and the balance of success rested decidedly with our opponents.

The massacre of the small garrison at Pulo Condore, which had been occupied because it was supposed to command the Gulf of Siam, was followed up by the fight in Pattania Harbour on the east coast of Malacca,—when Captain John Jourdan, President of the Indies, lost his life on board the "Sampson and Hound," which was assailed and defeated by a larger Dutch force. It is said that only three Englishmen escaped from the fray and that they made their way in a junk to Firando, our early settlement in Japan. Such was the implacability of the Dutch that they followed these fugitives to their place of retreat and demanded their surrender with menaces. But George Cock, the Governor of Firando, was a man of metal, and refused to yield one of his countrymen. He placed the factory in a position of defence, mounted ships' guns, and bade the Dutch do their worst. Then the Dutch invoked the intervention of the Japanese,—who like wise men retorted that the Europeans must settle their quarrels among themselves. As neither the Dutch nor the English wished to lose the Japan trade, no serious breach of the peace ensued.

The success at Pattania was followed by other naval victories, which added greatly to the Dutch reputation. The years 1618 and 1619 witnessed a general humiliation of the English in those seas. Captain Bonner and his ship the "Dragon," the same which figured in the first voyage as the "Scourge of the Sea," was sunk in one fight; the "Swan" and a second vessel were captured in another. The Dutch appear to have mastered one strategical principle, the bringing a preponderating force to bear on their adversary,—and the English vessels were destroyed or captured when left single-handed by want of judgment or over-confidence. But if the English ships were lost the factories remained and were bravely held. Polaroon and Lantore in the Moluccas, cut off from external communications by the loss of the ships named, were stoutly and successfully defended. The details in more durable form than letters home were never recorded, these contemporary manuscript records have perished, and all we know is that 32 of our countrymen on Polaroon baffled the Dutch in their full tide of triumph. Even under the gloom of Dutch prejudice and mastery there were gleams of the superior greatness of the future lords of the East.

When these calamities were commencing the East India Company had reinforced its fleet in the Archipelago and entrusted the supreme command to Sir Thomas Dale, but the new arrivals did not more than make up for the losses enumerated. Sir Thomas Dale arrived at a critical moment in the affairs of Java. The Native King of Bantam had taken umbrage at something the Dutch factors at Jacatra or Batavia had done, and he concluded an alliance with the English, who, nothing loth, attacked and destroyed the Dutch factory. This success was of transitory effect, for on the one side the King of Bantam did not wish to push the Dutch to extremities, and on the other the Dutch soon collected their forces, recovered Batavia, and renewed the contest of supremacy with increased forces and resolution.

At that juncture news arrived from Europe that a Treaty of Defence had been signed between the two States, and their representatives in the East were enjoined to live peaceably and act harmoniously together. These orders were received with external tokens of respect; salutes were fired, and the ships' yards were manned; but the contest had entered on too keen a stage to be arrested by orders dated six months before they could reach the field of rivalry. In the very year of their receipt, 1620, the Dutch retaliated for the attack on Batavia by driving the English out of Bantam, so that the object of the Treaty of Defence, the prevention of disputes between the English and Dutch, was defeated at the very commencement. After this temporary expulsion of the English from Bantam—they returned in 1628 and set up a subordinate factory—their chief station became Amboyna, in the Banda Isles. But even here the Dutch would not leave them alone. The fortunes of the English were at such a low ebb that it seemed to the Dutch that one bold stroke might place them in undisputed possession of the field.

The Dutch factory at Amboyna was stronger and held a larger garrison than the English. Mynheer Carpentier, the Governor-General of the Dutch Indies at Batavia, was a man of determination, and his subordinate at Amboyna had no scruples. The former was resolved to expel the English from the Archipelago, the latter saw a good opportunity of realising this desire by inventing a plot on the part of the English residents at Amboyna to overthrow the Dutch with the co-operation of the Japanese. With the view of proving the existence of this plot and at the same time to defeat it the Dutch lieutenant seized all the English at Amboyna. Their chief, Captain Gabriel Towerson, with nine English factors, nine Japanese and one Portuguese sailor, were all arrested, and some were tortured with the view of extracting a confession of conspiracy. This object having been attained, the ten Englishmen and their associates were executed on 17th February 1623, and the incident is very properly known to history as the Massacre of Amboyna. Carpentier refused to repudiate the act of his subordinate; no punishment was ever inflicted on the perpetrators of this barbarous act, and more than 30 years passed away before Cromwell obtained such reparation as compensation for some of the representatives of the victims could be deemed.

The Massacre of Amboyna raised a great outcry in England at the time, but it had more important consequences than its perpetrators foresaw. It established Dutch supremacy in the Eastern Archipelago; for in 1624 the English formally withdrew, and their subsequent efforts in this direction were made on a feebler and less extensive scale. But on the other hand it was this calamity that drove the English to make India the chief scene of their efforts to found a commercial supremacy. Several circumstances contributed to strengthen this resolution. If the Dutch were the victors in the Spice Islands, the English had signally triumphed over their other European rivals the Portuguese. In 1620 Captain Shillinge, after occupying Saldanha Bay at the Cape, and thus planting for the first time a European flag in South Africa, had sailed to Surat, defeating the Portuguese fleet in several encounters and further lowering their reputation among the Indians. But a still greater blow followed. In 1622 the island of Ormus, the seat of Portuguese power in the Persian Gulf since the time of Albuquerque, was captured by the English for the Persians; and although fighting continued for some years —in 1631 Swalley witnessed another serious encounter between English ships and the Viceroy of Goa's fleet—the Portuguese had ceased to be formidable before they signed a permanent treaty of peace with us in 1635.

These military successes had considerably increased the reputation of Englishmen along the coast of India, and had resulted in their obtaining many extra privileges from the Mogul's lieutenants. They were given authority by them, or by some of the still unsubdued kings of the Carnatic, to found factories at Agra and Patna in the north, and at Masulipatam and Armagon in the south. For a time Armagon, which is on the Coromandel coast, north of Madras, was the chief factory in India, its fort being defended by 12 guns, and the establishment consisting of 23 factors and soldiers. But the enumeration of these places, each of which signified a commercial and diplomatic success, is merely intended to show that the failure and humiliation of our merchant adventurers in the Archipelago were in marked contrast with the progress achieved in India itself. It is not surprising, therefore, that the operations and energy of our ancestors turned into the more profitable opening offered to them in the Mogul Empire, instead of to the islands where their Dutch rivals had established a firm foothold. The English may also be credited with having foreseen that the prizes offered by trade intercourse with a great and populous Empire like India must far exceed in value those to be wrested from the sparse populations of the Eastern Archipelago. The Amboyna Massacre marked the relaxation of our grasp on what may be called the Dutch Indies, but it was the determining cause which led to the concentration of our efforts on the mainland of India itself.

CHAPTER III.

THE GROWTH OF THE COMPANY.

ALTHOUGH the attention of the English was thus diverted from the Archipelago and concentrated as it were on India, it is proper to repeat that their only thought during the whole of the seventeenth century and for the first forty years of the eighteenth was to obtain trading facilities and factories by the favour of the great Mogul. The annals of the nascent East India Company are made up of the recorded establishment of their stations round the western and eastern coasts of the peninsula, and the fact that is most striking about their operations is that at one time or other they occupied and tested the merits of every possible port from Cambay on the one side to the Ganges on the other,—with of course the exception of Goa, then and still firmly held by the Portuguese as their metropolis in India. These factories were established as coigns of vantage not for purposes of conquest—no thought was more foreign or repugnant to the Company, which eventually became the most aggressive and conquering corporation the world has ever seen, than to play a *rôle* of high policy and aggrandisement—but as the best points for tapping the wealth of the interior. Many of them proved failures for the purpose with which they had been selected, the names of some are so completely forgotten that search in geographical dictionaries is necessary to identify them, but they one and all furnished evidence of the remarkable energy and persistency with which the English were pushing their trade with the chiefs and peoples of India. It was probably this systematic mode of proceeding which resulted in the fixed opinions of Maratha Chiefs and Mogul Governors that the English were a trading and not a fighting people.

Although factories had been set up at Patna and other places in the Gangetic valley in 1620 it was not till 1634 that a firman was given by the Emperor for trade in Bengal, and then it was restricted to such an inconvenient port—Pipli in Orissa—that the concession was practically of little value. Bengal, the milch cow of India, was at that time of such little importance in our eyes that it was placed under the restored presidency of Bantam in far off Java. In 1642 permission was given the English to remove their port of call from Pipli to Hughli in the Gangetic delta, and in 1645-6 further material concessions were made to them in this quarter owing to the services Dr. Gabriel Broughton had rendered in a medical capacity to the Emperor Shah Jehan. But the development of Bengal was very slow, and in 1658 it was made subordinate to Madras, which had in the meantime been established, in place of Bantam.

On the Coromandel coast the first station occupied was Masulipatam, and tacked on to this was a minor dependent factory at Armagon. In 1628 the former was abandoned and Armagon became the chief station on this coast. For its defence a corps of 20 soldiers, Englishmen recruited at home for Indian service, was raised and this is claimed as the stem from which the 1st European Madras (afterwards the 101st) Regiment sprang. Armagon itself was abandoned in 1638 as unsuited for commerce, and in 1639 Fort St. George at Madraspatam or Chineepatam was made the head factory on the coast of Coromandel. Fort St. George was occupied by the staff of the abandoned Armagon and received its garrison. It justified its selection, becoming in time the Presidential capital of Madras, but until 1683 it also was subordinate to the central administrative factory of Bantam.

On the west or Malabar coast Surat still

maintained its old supremacy, and even when Bombay was ceded to England as part of the dowry of Catherine of Braganza trade did not desert the old mart on the Taptee. Bombay, it must be noted, was obtained in a different manner from all our other possessions in India. The sovereign rights in that island were transferred to the King of England by another European monarch, and with the transfer we came for the first time into absolute possession of a portion of Indian territory. Charles the Second thought so little of his acquisition that in 1665 he assigned his rights over it to the East India Company in return for an annual payment of ten pounds. For a time it looked as if the King had accurately appraised the value of his cousin of Portugal's gift, for the Portuguese authorities refused to surrender the adjacent islet of Salsette, and for twenty years trade ignored the new emporium of Bombein, Bon Bay, or Bombay, which was a dependency of Surat until the year 1687.

It was during this period of uncertainty that one of the most memorable incidents in the early history of the English in India occurred, and as it was the first indication furnished to the natives that if the Company was all for peace its representatives could on occasion show themselves valiant men of war, it deserves special notice. The Moguls had not been firmly seated on the throne fifty years when the Hindus began to make efforts to shake off their authority, and in Central India the Marathas had found in Sivaji a leader worthy of their confidence and cause. His adventurous career must not turn our attention from our theme, for it only affects that in one incident. The wealth of Surat offered an attractive prize to a military chief seeking to draw followers to his standard and pressed by the difficulty of paying them when enlisted. Having overrun Malwa Sivaji made a descent on Surat in the year 1664, hoping not only to humble the Mogul Governor but to capture at a swoop the rich merchandise and treasures of the foreign merchants. Some tidings of the coming storm seems to have reached the ears of Sir George Oxenden, then "Governor of the English in India," for he called up guns and men from the anchorage at Swalley and placed the English factory at Surat in a good position of defence. When Sivaji arrived with his Maratha horde he had no difficulty in capturing the town, and in plundering its bazaar, the Parsee houses, and the Dutch factory, but when he reconnoitred the strong and well prepared position of the English, notwithstanding the inducement of its containing nearly £80,000 of merchandise, he drew off his forces, and our countrymen held their ground and property without firing scarcely a shot. It is said that Sivaji carried off with him spoil to the extent of one million sterling, but of that not sixpence was English. Sir George Oxenden's success stood him in good stead. The Mogul Emperor was vastly pleased at the check he had imposed on the progress of the formidable rebel Sivaji, and the English reputation rose in Western India at the expense of the Dutch and Portuguese.

In 1687 the Surat head factory was removed to Bombay, which thus became the centre and base of English power in Western India, just as Madras had become the English capital of Southern India 48 years earlier. In 1681 Bengal was released from its dependence on Madras, and in 1688, after many changes of site, the chief factory was fixed at Chuttanatee or Calcutta, where in the following year Fort William was erected in honour of the new king. Sir John Child was sent out from England with full powers to make peace or war with the Native Powers and to take charge of the Company's affairs as "Governor General"—a title that seems to have been only used in this isolated instance until conferred on Warren Hastings a century later. The three administrative divisions in India which exist at the present time were therefore well established before the close of the 17th century, and at the same time our merchants were finally expelled from Java by Dutch intrigues and violence.

The increased number of factories and fortified stations, the employment of a regular and increasing body of soldiers in the pay and subject to the orders of the Company, and perhaps also the discovery that the Mogul Empire was not quite so solid or substantial a creation as had been supposed, led some at least of the Company's representatives in India to form a larger conception of England's mission in that country. The secure possession of Bombay, free from the exactions of the ruling powers and from tyrannical interference by the Mogul governors, was also an incentive to acquire other positions in India on the same favourable conditions. It was at this time that ambitious schemes began to be entertained and perhaps discussed in the counting houses of the English factories, but they bore no fruit for another half century unless the following remarkable definition of policy expressed in 1689 in a letter of instructions sent out by the Court to its servants may be deemed such :—

"The increase of our *revenue* is the subject of our care as much as our trade; 'tis *that* must maintain our forces when twenty accidents may interrupt our trade, 'tis that must make us a nation in India; without that we are but a great number of interlopers united by his Majesty's Royal Charter, fit only to trade where nobody of power thinks it their interest to prevent us; and upon this account it is that the wise Dutch in all their general advices that we have seen write ten paragraphs concerning their Government, their civil and military policy, warfare and the increase of their revenue for one paragraph they write concerning trade."

The bolder attitude taken up by the Company towards the Native Powers was probably the cause of the conflicts that occurred in the first years of the settlement of Bengal, and amid which Calcutta was founded. The exactions of the Mogul's Governors increased; the native chiefs resorted to insults, one declaring that the "English were a company of base quarrelling people and foul dealers"; and at last the Company gave authority, if there was no other way out of the difficulty, to make war on the Mogul. In a letter of the Secret Committee received at Calcutta a few days after it was founded there occurs this remarkable passage:

"You must always understand that though we prepare for and resolve to enter into a warr with the Mogulls (being necessitated thereto) our ultimate end is peace for as we have never done it so our natures are most adverse to bloodshed and rapine which usually attend the most just warre. But we have no remedy left but either to desert our trade, or we must draw the sord his Majesty hath entrusted us with to vindicate the rights and honour of the English nation in India."

Hostilities actually took place. The Company's fleet captured several Mogul ships, and on Hidgley Island a regular engagement was fought. The English, twice repulsed in an attack on a native battery of 11 guns, carried it at the third attempt, when a Captain Arthburtnot—no doubt a misspelling for Arbuthnot—distinguished himself by leading his men to victory and spiking the guns. In this first battle of the English in Bengal, fought close to the scene of the more memorable Plassy, the Moguls left 60 killed on the ground, while our loss was two killed and two wounded. It was probably the discovery of the importance of Bengal, which was described by a contemporary as the "best flower in ye Company's garden," that led to this exceptional vigour, which was repaid by more than fifty years tranquillity in the Gangetic delta.

It was not only in the north that the English had to have recourse to arms to maintain their position. Several petty wars were fought in the neighbourhood of Fort St. David, the English neighbour of the French station of Pondicherry, but the details are not preserved. It is otherwise with the dramatic defence of Anjengo, the most southern of the English stations on the Malabar coast, which was in itself a most memorable occurrence and may be taken as typical of many another collision with the natives that has passed into oblivion. I give the account as contained in the manuscript record which alone preserves the incident:—

"A war ensued and several skirmishes happened 'twixt the English and the natives, but the former always gaining the better a cessation of arms was agreed on and remained so till Mr. Walter Brown (of Council of Bombay) arrived at Anjenga, who brought matters to such an issue that it was agreed upon—viz., so soon as ever the customary annual allowance to the Queen and Poolar was paid that all disputes should be laid in oblivion. Now the unhappy affair works to a period. No sooner was Mr. Brown gone off the place but Mr. Gyfford, flushed with the hopes of having peace and pepper and the more to ingratiate himself with the country government, thought he could not send those presents in too pompous a manner. Therefore he musters all the English menial servants, many of the inhabitants, and all the flower of the garrison, and marches on a fixed day to the Queen's Palace at Attinga with as little concern as to take the air, leaving none but a few invalids for the defence of the fort (the most preposterous and unprecedented action as ever was heard of). On their arrival at Attinga they found a great conflux of the natives ready to receive them, and as the custom of the country arm'd, which, however, at first did not give room for the English to suspect there was such a damnable treason on foot, but rather that they were come to be spectators.

"As I have said, on their arrival at Attinga Mr. Cowse was pitched upon to go and consult with the chief men how to behave in the delivery of the presents, whom it was necessary to gratify at such a juncture, and what sum to each person of distinction. It was at this consultation that Mr. Cowse imagin'd there was some evil on foot because of the whispers and delays on the part of the Mallabars, upon which he was very pressing with Mr. Gyfford to return, who was deaf to all his entreatys. During the interim some of the most active of the commonalty secures the ammunition, which no sooner was known (than) the Caraccars first and then the mob in general rushed on our people who were drawn up in an enclosure, and in a manner pounded were soon overcome. Messrs. Gyfford, Burton, Fleming and some others of the English was tortured very much, and the linguist dismembered gradually that he might feel the greater torment. Mr. Cowse luckily got out of the crowd on the first onset, disguising himself in the country habit, hoping thereby to escape. But when they had made an end of killing nigh two hundred souls, the murtherers made directly to the fort, and in the way a Moor merchant in company of others accidentally taking the path Mr. Cowse did (and to whom the former was largely indebted) he was discovered and kill'd to quit scores, notwithstanding all the assurance man could give that he freely acquitted him (the Moor) of all he owed to spare his life, but so it was resolved for stone dead has no fellow."

Such was the catastrophe at Attinga when 200 Englishmen and their servants lost their lives. Strangely enough the whole episode had passed into oblivion until my discovery some years ago of the contemporary evidence among the India Office records. But if the natives had massacred the English colony the valour and energy of one Englishman, the gunner Ince, saved the fort, and I continue the story in the words of the original narrator:—"Three of the Topasses (much wounded) and a Christian boy or two were the first that gave notice to the fort of the misfortune. Upon which the gunner Ince, with the ablest of those invalids Mr. Gyfford had left to guard the fort and by the assistance of the souldiers' wives, directly carry'd provisions from the Bank Sal to the fort, and secured themselves ere the country people made any attempt. But their arrival was soon enough to terrify those handful of men was in the fort. The gunner, a man of true courage and prudence, did wonders on this emergency by animating those with him to make a vigorous defence, even to blow up the magazine and perish that way rather than fall into the enemy's hands. And to his praise be it spoken, as often as the enemy attempted the fort (which they did several times, thinking themselves so fine of carrying their design that they endeavoured to scale it) he as often repulsed them, killing a considerable number of the enemy, which so discouraged them that they quitted their design on the fort and fell to plundering and burning the Limitts. However the fort and Bank Sal was defended upwards of five months with great resolution and bravery, more especially considering it was then the monsoon time and by daily alarms from the enemy our people almost harassed to death, and at last must certainly have fallen into their hands had not the vigilance of that worthy gentleman Mr. Adams, Chief of Tillicherry, sent them a succour of men and provisions, through which timely assistance without dispute the Honourable Company owe the enjoying Anjenga Fort at this juncture."

These incidents will suffice to prove that from the very beginning of its career in the East the English Company had to show that it could stand up for its rights and that it was ready if no alternative course offered itself to draw the sword even against the Mogul. One cause of this increased confidence was no doubt the possession of more accurate knowledge as to the Emperor's power, and at the end of the 17th century the Mogul Empire occupied a much lower position in the estimation of Englishmen than it had at the beginning. Aurungzebe was not Akbar or even Jehangir, and it was well known that the principal of his generals had set up an independent dynasty at Hyderabad, in the Deccan. What has been written may serve as a corrective for the narrow but hitherto generally accepted view that the French pointed out to us the way to conquest in India. Englishmen are too apt to consider that English exploit in the East began with Clive and that but for Dupleix we should have nothing in our Asiatic enterprises worthy of the notice of history. The truth is very different, for the whole of the 17th century was marked by many noteworthy deeds, referred to in this and the preceding chapter, as well as by a persevering energy in overcoming obstacles and a consistent policy without which it is scarcely too much to say that Clive's achievements would not have borne fruit.

At this stage it will be convenient to record briefly the names of the various companies or associations, all of which were finally merged in 1708-9 into the United Company which constituted the famous association known to history that disappeared in 1857. The London Company which received its Charter from Elizabeth is rightly regarded as the Parent stem, and the achievements we have recorded were performed by its servants. In 1635 a new association named Courten's was founded by the favour of

Charles the 1st, but in 1650 it was absorbed by the London Company. For the first years of its existence it was very energetic, but its captains acted more like buccaneers than peaceful traders. One of these, Captain Weddell, sailed up the Canton River, and when the Chinese authorities showed their customary obstructive tactics he at once resorted to strong measures. He landed his men, captured a fort, and seized what he required.

Another chartered association, called the Merchant Adventurers, was founded in 1655, but it was united with the head Company within two years. The last, known as the English Company, was incorporated in 1698 and promised to prove a most formidable rival to the London Company, which had spent £90,000 in bribing the Privy Council to renew its own Charter and to withhold one from its rival. Evelyn in his diary says the London Company lost the day by only ten votes in Parliament, and that because "so many of its friends were absent to see a tiger baited by dogs." Baffled in one direction, a solution was found in another by the negotiations which commenced in 1702 and concluded in 1709 for the union of the two companies, whose path was thenceforward the same and whose only rivals were not their fellow-countrymen but their national enemies.

The East India Company was a close

corporation, and strongly resented any encroachment on its rights, even when the rival associations had royal or Parliamentary authority. How much more did it resent the competition of adventurous individuals who traded without any authority but their own courage and confidence. These men were called Interlopers, and the Company pursued them in the East with sword and imprisonment, in London with fines and other legal penalties, as only the powerful can oppress the weak. They were denounced as rats and treated as vermin, yet the national character was as well vindicated by their reckless bravery as by the systematic but more selfish proceedings of the Company's servants. We can only refer to the greatest of all the Interlopers, Thomas Pitt, the founder of the family which gave England two of her proudest names. For twenty years of his life he was the terror of the East India Company. He was a "desperate fellow," the leader of the Interlopers, a man to be hunted down whenever found. Fined in London, imprisoned in India, he still sailed his ship under the nose of the Company's squadrons, and sold his goods on the London market in despite of the Honourable Court, for he was "cool in action, saw what to do and did it." At length admiration or helplessness suggested another course. Thomas Pitt, having expended some part of his Indian profits in gaining a seat in Parliament, was taken into the Company's service, and sent out as President of Fort St. George at Madras. For more than ten years he governed that important possession to the profit of the Company and the enhancement of his own credit, being known as "The Great President" or "The Great Pits."

He was a worthy predecessor of the great men who followed, from Clive to the Lawrences—all servants of the Company, and all makers of British India. Yet his name has been preserved, not for what he accomplished, but partly because he was the grandfather of Chatham and the ancestor of the Great Commoner, and chiefly because he brought the famous Pitt or Regent diamond to England. Among his original methods in dealing with Indian trade was that which he adopted in the matter of home remittances. Wishing to make them in the simplest and most compact form, he fixed on diamonds. He must have been a sound judge of the stone and a shrewd dealer to have got the better of the native gem merchant. Among his purchases he bought a large stone of 410 carats for £12,500. He had it recut on his return, and when reduced to 137 carats it was valued at twelve times the price he gave for it. The transaction was a big one for those days, but neither his courage nor his judgment can be impugned. For some years he wore the stone as an ornament, and his picture was painted with the gem fixed in his hat. The fame of the stone became European, and the Regent of France, the Duke of Orleans, expressed a desire to become its purchaser. Long negotiations ensued, and at last, in 1717, the stone was sent to France on the receipt of security in two boxes of gems, and on the understanding that £135,000 should be paid for it. There is reason to think that the money was never paid, but the security may have sufficed. Seventy-five years later the Pitt or Regent diamond was valued in France at half a million sterling.

For thirty years after the departure of Pitt the history of the East India Company was uneventful. It strengthened its position in the many factories it held round the coast, it extended its trade operations, it earned greater dividends; but there were fewer incidents, and the political functions of the Presidents and their staff were merged in their commercial pursuits. The rivalry of the Portuguese and Dutch had been practically overcome, and so long as the native Powers were not too exacting there was no call for special energy or self-assertion. Things were in this tranquil state when a new and more formidable rival appeared on the scene and threatened us with the loss of all we had built up during a century and a-half of sustained if silent effort.

CHAPTER IV.

OUR RIVALRY WITH FRANCE.

IF rivalry with the Portuguese and Dutch marked the early period of English enterprise in India, the more serious rivalry and struggle with France that followed will always attract greater historical attention because it was associated with the first assertion of British political and military power in the peninsula. That assertion would inevitably have come sooner or later. Sixty years before the French won the battle of St. Thomé the English had fearlessly thrown down the gage to the Mogul himself and defeated his armies. Only a qualified assent can therefore be given to the view eloquently expressed by Macaulay and Malleson that Dupleix pointed out for our ancestors the road to conquest in India. If Dupleix could have controlled the sea as at one moment he did control the Carnatic everything would have been possible for France, but without that mastery the successes of her great representative were always hollow and ephemeral. Apart from the question of naval superiority the resources which England possessed in India were immeasurably greater than those of France, owing first of all to England having had a start of her neighbour of over eighty years and secondly to the energy and enterprise with which the East India Company pushed its undertakings as compared with the French Company. Behind the former was a people resolute to extend its trade while the latter could only depend on the personal and passing support of an occasional Minister of France. At the moment of the commencement of the struggle there were ten English factories in India for one French; where one French ship rounded the Cape twenty English could be counted, and, as Dupleix himself admitted, Madras overshadowed Pondicherry and the English held all the best places for trade.

The first French attempt to trade with India is said to have been made in 1603, when the City of Rouen fitted out two ships. The expedition resulted in failure and loss. In 1642 Richelieu founded the first French East India Company. It was not successful, and Colbert is entitled to the credit of having launched the enterprise in a more successful and conspicuous manner. He gave the company an extended charter and financial support. His representative, Caron, became the first Governor of Pondicherry, and although the French got a bad name for leaving Surat without paying their debts they made good their position on the Coromandel coast and a few years later at Chandernagore in the delta of the Ganges. François Martin and his successor Lenoir were able administrators and in every way a credit to their country, and in their hands Pondicherry made as much progress as could have been expected. Chandernagore on the other hand languished, and Dupleix first made his reputation as an administrator by the extraordinary improvement he effected in its condition during his intendantship from 1730 to 1741. In the latter year Dupleix was rewarded for his skill and success in Bengal with the supreme control of French India as Governor of Pondicherry.

The French were not very energetic or very successful traders at their most flourishing epoch, but they were more affable in their manners to the natives and more considerate towards their prejudices and customs than it can be said the English were then or indeed are now. Their relations with the native chiefs were consequently of an agreeable nature and conveyed the idea of an influence and power which were mainly on the surface. Still they cannot be described as altogether barren, for in 1736 Governor Dumas obtained from the Governor of the Carnatic the right, subsequently confirmed by the Emperor of Delhi, to coin the gold and silver money for his provinces. This was a task specially suited to French skill and was no doubt performed with mutual satisfaction, for if the Moguls obtained a handsome and intrinsically valuable currency the French cleared an annual profit of one hundred thousand pounds, which represented the cargoes of many vessels. The Indian connection was therefore not altogether valueless to France, and there seems to have been during those early years a complete absence of that spirit of rivalry between the French and the English which had characterised our relations with the Portuguese and the Dutch. The explanation may have been that the French were never in a position to attempt rivalry with us in matters of trade. Whatever the reason, the fact remains indisputable that until the outbreak of the war of the Austrian succession in 1742 there had been no conflict between the two nations in India.

When news of that war reached India, Dupleix, fully alive to the inferiority of his position as compared with the English, made a proposition to Governor Morse of Madras that the hostilities in progress in Europe should not be extended to India and that there should be abstention from all warfare between Madras and Pondicherry. Governor Morse, not less aware than Dupleix of his superiority, declined to tie his hands by any such understanding. In this difficulty Dupleix appealed to Anwar-ud-Din, Governor of the Carnatic, who was induced by goodwill to the French or more probably for his own reasons to send Governor Morse a peremptory order to the effect that he would not allow the Europeans to fight with one another on the soil of India. As this representative of the Mogul possessed an army capable of enforcing his orders compliance was the only course open to the English Governor.

This precautionary measure was taken by Dupleix before the war had actually commenced, but as he knew that Anwar-ud-Din's order would not apply to the sea he took such steps as were within his power to avert his being cut off from Europe. At the moment an English squadron commanded the approach round Ceylon, and Dupleix had no ships or expectation of ships from Europe wherewith to combat them. In these circumstances he made strong representations for assistance to La Bourdonnais, the Governor of Mauritius, who had distinguished himself when a young man by the capture of Mahé, the third French possession in India, and who had at a later period raised the civil and military administration of Mauritius to a high state of efficiency. La Bourdonnais was not deaf to those messages, but several years were occupied first in making the French position in his own island secure against a sudden attack and secondly in equipping something approaching a fighting squadron from unpromising and insufficient materials. It was not until 1746 that these necessary preliminaries were completed and La Bourdonnais sailed for French India.

As his fleet although numerically equal was inferior in armament to the English squadron under Commodore Peyton, the best chance of the French leader to reach Pondicherry seemed to lie in his evading the enemy; but the English watch was good, and if their courage had matched it the ambitious projects of Dupleix would never have emerged from the stage of conception. The two fleets engaged, and after a desultory fight, which the English commander had only to press home to convert into a decisive victory, La Bourdonnais was allowed to continue his voyage unmolested to Pondicherry, while the English ships withdrew to a safe anchorage on the northern coast of Sumatra. It was not a day of which our navy had reason to be proud, for Commodore Peyton's retreat left Madras at the mercy of the French.

The arrival of La Bourdonnais with his ships and the considerable body of troops they had on board promised Dupleix the triumph he had contemplated over the English. In the early stage of the war he had saved himself from being overwhelmed by invoking the intervention of the Mogul Governor, but now that he was ready to assume the offensive he paid no heed to the other side of that functionary's order that the Europeans were not to engage in hostilities. The execution of his scheme for the destruction of the English at Madras was delayed by differences with his colleague which at last culminated in an open rupture, but before that occurred La Bourdonnais left to attack Madras by land and sea. The English position was not a strong one, and no adequate preparations had been made to stand a siege. In his difficulty Governor Morse sent a mission to the Governor of the Carnatic requesting him to order the French to retire. Anwar-ud-Din would not send the order, and the French batteries opened fire on Fort St. George. In a few days Governor Morse seeing no alternative surrendered and the French occupied the place. Negotiations were then entered into between Morse and La Bourdonnais for the ransom of the town, and, notwithstanding the protests and opposition of Dupleix, were concluded with that object. There is no doubt that La Bourdonnais was induced to concede these favourable terms to the English by the receipt of a large bribe, but in one respect our representatives miscalculated for they could not compel the French commander to remain to carry out his agreement. La Bourdonnais was most anxious to leave the coast before the outbreak of the monsoon, a terrible storm shattered his vessels and cost the lives of 1,200 soldiers, and in a moment of consternation or despair he hastened on board his ship and left the coast, which he declared he wished he had not seen.

After his colleague's departure Dupleix refused to recognise the ransom of Madras, and his troops remained in that place. The Mogul Governor had refused Morse's request to stop the French advance, but he was ill-pleased at the magnitude of their success, and when he found them retaining possession of Madras he sent an order to restore it to the English and followed up his message by despatching an army to give it effect. Dupleix, undismayed by this threat, held on to his prize and sent all the troops he could collect under the command of an experienced Swiss soldier named Paradis to encounter the Mogul army. The two forces met at St. Thomé, and the Moguls were routed. Then was shown for the first time what a small disciplined body of European troops could accomplish against native untrained masses although possessing a numerical superiority of twenty to one. Encouraged by that success Dupleix openly repudiated the ransom of Madras, which up to that moment he had only ignored. Some of the English residents hearing this escaped from Madras to Fort St. David, and one of the number was Robert Clive.

Dupleix resolved to add Fort St. David to his conquests; and as the Governor of the Carnatic, impressed by the French victories, abandoned the English, there seemed every reason to anticipate his success. The Fort St. David garrison however made a stout defence, and repulsed two attacks, one led by Paradis, the victor of St. Thomé. The chances of ultimate success were still on the side of the French when the arrival of a fresh English fleet under Admiral Griffin saved Fort St. David and restored the equality of the struggle. Major Stringer Lawrence also arrived to take the command of the Company's forces, and obtained a success at Gudalore in January 1748, which was however neutralised by his being taken prisoner while besieging Ariakuram. The English forces were further increased by the arrival of Admiral Boscawen, and an expedition was fitted out to attack the French in Pondicherry as a set off for the loss of Madras, which still remained in their hands. Dupleix and his lieutenant Paradis, who was killed in a sortie, made a gallant and successful defence, and after six weeks Admiral Boscawen, whose skill on land was not equal to his capacity at sea, was constrained to order a retreat, with a loss of one thousand of his men during the siege. Before the struggle could be renewed intelligence arrived of the signing of the Treaty of Aix la Chapelle. Dupleix restored Madras, and a truce obtained in the struggle between France and England on the Coast of Coromandel.

Compelled by the peace to forego his projects for the discomfiture of the English, Dupleix turned his attention to the task of aggrandisement by taking a side in the intrigues and strife of the several native chiefs of Southern India. This was no new departure, for in the time of M. Dumas the French had given shelter to the widow of the ruler of the Carnatic after her husband had fallen in battle with the Marathas. It was at that time too that the French first established an influence over Chunda Sahib, the nephew of that potentate. In 1741 Chunda Sahib was taken prisoner by the Marathas and carried off to Sattara. There he remained until Dupleix in 1849, turning over his schemes for establishing French supremacy, bethought him that he might prove a useful puppet and sent the amount of his ransom to Sattara. Chunda

Sahib was released and by the aid of a French force under Bussy recovered Arcot and the titular position as ruler of the Carnatic. At the same time Dupleix took up the cause of Muzaffir Jung as Subahdar of the Deccan, so that France was for the moment a political power, whereas the English on the conclusion of peace seemed to have returned to their commercial pursuits and laid aside their swords. Within a year of Dupleix's bare escape at the hands of Admiral Boscawen he had made himself the apparent arbiter of the Deccan, and had been rewarded by his native allies with titles, presents, and territorial possessions. This moment, when the two principal rulers of Southern India were the sworn allies and personal debtors of Dupleix, represented the high water mark of French power in India.

The French position had scarcely been thus fairly established when it began to perceptibly weaken. In 1751, one year after his succession to the Subahdarship of the Deccan, Muzaffir Jung died. The French were bound to support as his successor Salabat Jung, an ardent admirer of themselves. The English, stirred by an instinct of self-preservation as well as rivalry, recognised Mahomed Ali, and his title was certainly the better, but as the English were assumed to have no military power their support seemed but a weak reed to lean on.

The defeat of a small English force at Volconda, when Clive was present, pointed to the triumph of the French and their nominees. Chunda Sahib had recovered Arcot, and was now engaged in the siege of Trichinopoli, held by a small English force, which was reduced to the lowest straits when the repulse of the relieving expedition at Volconda seemed to seal its fate. It was the lowest point reached by English fortune during these years of unceasing struggle.

At this juncture a man of genius and a born leader of men appeared on the scene in the person of Robert Clive, and gave the whole struggle a different course. Robert Clive had reached India in 1744 as a youth of seventeen. The restraint and dull routine of a commercial life were distasteful to him, but he played a manly part in the defence of Madras, from which he made his escape when Dupleix refused to carry out the terms of the ransom. In May 1747 he was given at his own request an ensign's commission at Fort St. David, because he was "of a martial disposition." He showed himself active and dutiful in his new profession, gaining the good opinion of Major Stringer Lawrence, but it was not until the repulse at Volconda that he came to the front. After that reverse he hastened to Madras, and, representing to Mr. Saunders the Governor that

Trichinopoli must fall when the French triumph would be assured, unless some prompt measures of rescue were adopted, drew up a plan for carrying the war into the enemy's country by attacking Arcot and thus drawing off some of the troops before Trichinopoli. The proposer of this bold scheme was a young man of twenty-four who had never had any military training, and it is not going too far to say that from the majority of governors he would have received an absolute and probably a sneering rejection of his proposal as impracticable and visionary. Fortunately Mr. Saunders was a man of broad views and free from prejudice. He saw the advantage of the plan and he did not sneer at the youth or want of experience of its proposer. He placed a small force of 200 Englishmen and 300 natives at Clive's orders and promised him every support in his power.

Clive marched on and occupied Arcot without opposition, but the French did not relax their efforts before Trichinopoli and for the moment it looked as if the main object of his move would fail. But Chunda Sahib could not acquiesce in even the temporary loss of his chief city, and he drew off a considerable portion of his own army to recover it, with the help of a small French contingent. As Clive's force had been reduced by sickness to little more than half its original strength the destruction of the English seemed inevitable. Clive, however, had made skilful preparations for defence, and after seven weeks' resistance he had the satisfaction of defeating the final assault of Chunda Sahib's army. The success was rendered the more remarkable because it led the Maratha chief Morari Rao, who thought the French triumph assured, to take the field and fulfil his engagements to Mahomed Ali.

If Clive's defence of Arcot was creditable, his military genius was revealed more clearly in the promptitude with which he followed up his success. His patron Saunders, delighted at the success of an experiment in which his own reputation was involved, sent him as many troops as he could raise—200 Europeans and 700 natives. With these, and supported by Morari Rao's irregular cavalry, Clive advanced to attack Chunda Sahib's army, which had been reinforced by a further French contingent and occupied a strong position on the Arni. He gained a complete victory, and for the first time a French force had to leave an open field in the possession of the English. The success was the more gratifying because there were as many Frenchmen as Englishmen engaged in the battle. Other successes followed, but perhaps the most notable of them was the destruction of the city and monument which the French Governor had created in the plenitude of his power and named Dupleix Fattehabad, or City of the

Victory of Dupleix. As the campaign for the new year 1752 was about to commence Major Lawrence returned from Europe to take up the command, and as Clive's health had broken down he sailed for England, after adding two fresh military triumphs to his list in the capture of the forts of Covelong and Chingleput. The relations between these two comrades in arms were excellent, and in strong contrast with those between Dupleix and his chief subordinates. Lawrence called Clive "a man of an undaunted resolution, of a cool temper and of a presence of mind which never left him in the greatest danger—born a soldier"; and Clive, mindful of the consideration this soldier by profession had shown him, refused the jewelled sword offered him by the Company on his arrival in London unless a similar one was given to his chief and friend Major Stringer Lawrence.

The campaign of 1752-3 was a remarkable one and led to the fall of Dupleix. Lawrence gained in the earlier year a considerable success at Bahur over the French, Chunda Sahib was taken prisoner and executed, and Dupleix made a fatal mistake in allowing his one capable officer, Bussy, to leave the Coromandel coast for Aurungabad, on the other side of India. When the struggle was resumed in 1753 Dupleix made a supreme effort to restore the fortune of war by the capture of

Trichinopoli, and Lawrence covered that place with his small force. The manœuvres which took place on the banks of the Cauvery occupied a period of months, during which Lawrence won three separate battles. It was not until the decisive repulse of Mainville's attempt to capture Trichinopoli by a *coup de main* that Dupleix resigned himself to defeat and recalled his beaten troops. It was almost his last act of authority. A few months later he was recalled by his own Government, which had been induced to concur with the English representations that the ambition of Dupleix formed the only obstacle to pacific relations between the two countries in India. An ungrateful country put this able statesman on his trial and prosecuted him till the day of his death in penury and grief.

When France recalled Dupleix in 1754 the outlook in Europe was peaceful. Two years later the Seven Years War began, and France and England took opposite sides. The French then reverted to some of their old plans, not for founding an Indian Empire but for injuring their adversary in the east. An expedition composed of two veteran and distinguished regiments, those of Lally and Lorraine, was fitted out in 1757 and placed under the command of Lally Tollendal, a gallant and experienced soldier whose desperate courage and quick decision at the head of part of the

Irish Brigade had turned Fontenoy from a defeat into the most brilliant victory the French ever gained over an English army. As the son of an Irish chieftain who had left his native country after the surrender of Limerick he was animated by a special hostility to the English, and he threw himself with extraordinary energy and zeal into the task of overthrowing his hereditary enemies. He was joined soon after his arrival by Bussy, who was the military director of the Subahdar of the Deccan—or the Nizam, as he soon began to be called—but Bussy, although experienced in Indian warfare, had not the same professional skill or honesty as Lally. Bussy was envious of the greater fame of his colleague, and Lally formed unfortunately the lowest opinion of Bussy and of everyone else associated with India. His own operations were conducted in a vigorous and daring manner that had not been seen in India except when Clive was present, and Clive was in Bengal heavily engaged in securing the new possessions. Lally sat down before Fort St. David and captured it. He laid siege to Madras, and the English emporium seemed on the eve of a second surrender. Troops were sent from Bengal under the command of Eyre Coote, and a fleet hastily assembled under Admiral Pocock brought the French covering squadron under D'Aché to an action and defeated it on 10th September 1759.

But the decisive engagement had to be fought on land and not at sea. Sir Eyre Coote had a force of nearly 2,000 Europeans and over 3,000 natives. The French commanders had 1,500 Europeans and 4,000 natives. Lally and Bussy, although not in close accord, were two brave and capable officers, and when the rival armies faced each other on the field of Wandiwash on 21st January 1760 no one could have confidently predicted the result. Although both armies contained a considerable number of natives they took little or no part in the action, which was almost entirely restricted to the Europeans. Lally's position was a strong one, with his left resting on a hill crowned by a battery manned by sailors, and on his right he placed his European cavalry, 150 in number. He decided to commence the action with a cavalry charge, in the hope of turning the English left and assisting his main infantry attack from the centre. Placing himself at the head of the cavalry he sounded the charge, but the men refused to follow him. It was only at the third attempt that they could be induced to charge, and then in a faint-hearted manner. In the meantime the battle became general and an accidental shot caused the explosion of a powder magazine on the hill, which killed 80 of the sailors and destroyed the position. Notwithstanding this misfortune and the capture of Bussy, Lally made a strenuous resistance, and for a moment it seemed as if he might have inflicted on the English in India almost as severe a defeat as he had been the chief cause of bringing about in Europe. It was not to be, however, and all he succeeded in doing was to prolong the struggle by the vigorous defence of Pondicherry until January 7th 1761. In that month the French capital surrendered, the remnants of the regiments of Lally and Lorraine, with their gallant leader, were allowed to leave the country, and the English supremacy was placed beyond question. In 1766, Lally, despite the petition of the Duke de Soubise in the name of the French Army that his life might be spared, was executed, and three years later the French East India Company was allowed to expire, as all hopes of the resuscitation of French power had been extinguished.

Although our rivalry with France may be said to have been settled on the field of Wandiwash, two incidents of a later date claim brief notice under the same head. It is true that the French pretensions to vie with us on anything like terms of equality ended with Lally's defeat, but individual Frenchmen kept alive for a time the tradition of the military prowess of the Grande Nation. Bussy and Raymond at the Nizam's court, and De Boigne at Scindiah's, were the most famous of these organisers of armies, but they had many successors more or less capable down to the fall of the Sikh system in 1849. In 1780 the French made a second attempt to injure the English in India. Encouraged by the growth of Hyder Ali's power and by reports that the English were hard beset by the double wars with Mysore and the Marathas, the French Government despatched a fleet to the Indian ocean, first under D'Owis and subsequently under the able Suffren. The English men-of-war as well as traders suffered much at their hands, especially from Suffren, who anticipated some of Nelson's tactics—in particular the principle of "laying your enemy by the board." But these naval successes were ephemeral. They did not give a correct idea of the relative power of the two navies, and after two years of doubt and anxiety Suffren was constrained to return to Europe and the captains of the Company's argosies again breathed freely on their voyage home.

But on land the period of doubt and anxiety did not last so long. In 1780 the reports of the progress of Hyder Ali's army and of the gross mismanagement of the Madras authorities alarmed Warren Hastings, then Governor general at Calcutta. With characteristic promptitude he decided to sen the best officer at his disposal to dismiss the incompetent Governor of Madras by an assertion of authority in excess of the written letter of his warrant.

He induced Sir Eyre Coote, the victor of Wandiwash twenty years before, to take the command, although the force placed at his disposal was very meagre and scarcely exceeded that with which he had defeated Lally. When Coote reached Madras in November 1780 he found the French fleet in possession of the roadstead, the town of Wandiwash on the eve of surrender to Hyder Ali, and a state of panic prevailing at Fort St. George. The most important step was to draw Hyder Ali away from Madras, and to relieve Wandiwash. With this object Coote executed a difficult march to the south of Pondicherry, but although he succeeded in his main object he found he had placed himself in a disadvantageous and dangerous position in face of Hyder Ali's numerous army, with which the French squadron was able to co-operate. When he reached Cuddalore, a short distance south of Pondicherry, he endeavoured to recover the ground he had lost by assuming the offensive, but in an attack on the Pagoda of Chelambakam he suffered a repulse which might have had grave consequences. It was then that he retired a few miles further south and took up a strong position at Porto Novo. The spirit of this gallant general, untamed by years or by his recent reverse, would not brook a defensive battle. He again assumed the offensive and inflicted on Hyder Ali as crushing a defeat as any recorded in Anglo-Indian history. He followed up his success on the field with remarkable energy and without leaving his enemy time to breathe. When he halted his small army in February 1782 he had in little more than twelve months rescued the whole of the Madras Presidency from a confident and daring assailant, and inflicted a succession of defeats on the ablest native soldier and ruler Southern India had ever known.

The French expedition to Egypt under Napoleon Bonaparte in 1798 was part of a general project to assist Tippoo Sultan, son of Hyder Ali, in his last struggle with the English. The reply to that menace was Nelson's victory of the Nile, the battle of Aboukir, the capture of Seringapatam and General Baird's expedition from India to Egypt. In 1808-9 Napoleon made a fresh effort to harass our commerce and to establish a new base in Java. His ships after doing some mischief to our commerce were destroyed; Java, at the instigation of Sir Stamford Raffles, was conquered and held for a period of years; and with these incidents the name of France finally disappeared from the scene of competition in India. It is only of late years that it has reappeared further East in Indo-China, where some enthusiasts dream of executing the projects of Dupleix.

CHAPTER V.

THE CONQUEST OF INDIA.

THE conquest of India by the East India Company began with the struggle with the French, but this, although the opening incident, did not long occupy the stage, and even before Lally made his effort to restore the fortunes of his country the foundation of the British dominion in India had been securely laid. Mention was made in the last chapter that soon after his first successes Clive was compelled by ill health to leave for home, and the closing operations with Dupleix were conducted by Stringer Lawrence and others. Three years' stay in England sufficed to restore Clive's health, exhaust his savings, and make him willing to again enter on active work. In 1755 he sailed for India as Governor of Fort St. David, and with the military rank of Lieutenant-Colonel conferred on him by George the Second. On his way out he turned aside to attack, with the co-operation of Admiral Watson, the piratical stronghold of Gheriah, held by the Maratha chief Angria, who had successfully defied the Bombay authorities and whose raids extended as far as the Persian Gulf and the Red Sea. This enterprise was crowned with complete success. Angria's fleet was destroyed, his fortress captured and dismantled, and his treasure—valued at £150,000—divided among the victors. With this addition to his laurels Clive arrived to take up his post at Fort St. David.

The lull in events in Madras was broken upon by the receipt of startling news from Bengal a few weeks after Clive's arrival on the coast of Coromandel. That great province had been quite unaffected by the events in the southern and senior presidency. The French held Chandernagore, but there was no contest between that place and Calcutta in imitation of the struggle between Madras and Pondicherry. Still, the tendency to regard Bengal as "the fairest flower in the Company's garden," noted in an earlier epoch, had been strengthened by the increase of the trade in the Gangetic delta and by its exceptionally profitable character. But on the other hand the Mogul Viceroy of Bengal was supposed to wield a far superior military power to that possessed by any of the southern satraps. Behind his deputy at Moorshedabad stood the great Emperor himself on the throne of Delhi, and, diminished as was the respect paid in Madras to the mere numbers of the native armies, it was still otherwise in Bengal. Moreover it is only fair to note that the establishment at Calcutta was a civil and commercial one, whereas that at Madras had assumed an essentially military character with its European regiments and thousands of trained Sepoys. Surprise should not be felt therefore at the attitude of the Calcutta authorities being more respectful and even servile towards the native rulers than that of their colleagues in Madras, where victories easily won by Frenchmen and Englishmen over countless masses of natives had taught a correct appreciation of the superiority of discipline over numbers.

The events that led to the establishment of British power on the Ganges can in no wise be attributed to the arrogance or self-assertion of the East India Company's representatives. Their policy was peace, and they would submit to any exactions short of absolute repression and extortion. There is absolutely no evidence to warrant the charge that Mr. Holwell and his colleagues had any political designs, and they must be wholly acquitted of having contributed in any way to the hostile and tyrannical proceedings of the Viceroy of Bengal, Surajah Dowlah.

That youthful potentate succeeded his grandfather at the early age of twenty almost at the moment of Clive's return to India. It is said that he hated the English from his childhood,—a statement as hard to prove as to disprove,—and that he gave himself up to the worst forms of brutal debauchery. It is certain that if there had never been a Black Hole tragedy his name would long ere this have passed into oblivion. Taking offence at several trifling matters which he interpreted as infringing his dignity and authority, Surajah Dowlah marched with a large army upon Calcutta. It must be admitted that the English there showed great pusillanimity, and acted after a very different fashion from stout Job Charnock and Captain Arbuthnot who stormed the Mogul battery 70 years earlier. The Governor fled to the ships, and the ships sailed down the Hughli leaving Fort William to surrender at discretion. Surajah Dowlah entered the British factory and summoned the English prisoners into his presence. They were 146 in number and Mr. Holwell, Member of Council, was the chief of them. The Viceroy abused them in language made more forcible by disappointment at having found so little treasure, but he promised them their lives and there is no reason to suppose that he did not intend to keep his word. In fact his greed would have impelled him to do so, as he might look for a substantial ransom from their fellow-countrymen. But unfortunately for himself and his ill-fated prisoners he retired from the room without giving any orders for their disposal, and some cruel and careless subordinate forced these 146 Europeans into the room, twenty feet square, which had been used to incarcerate the occasional prisoners of the factory, and which was familiarly designated the Black Hole. The officials who perpetrated this act of cruelty refused to repair it by asking the Nabob for final orders, on the ground that he was asleep and could not be disturbed. In the morning the Nabob gave orders for their release, but 123 of the captives were dead, and several of the surviving 23 died later, or never recovered their reason.

It is unnecessary to dwell on the painful and terrible incidents of this tragedy. When the tidings reached Madras there went up a cry for vengeance such as was heard a century later under very similar circumstances at Cawnpore, and Clive was on the spot to execute a mission imposed on him as much by outraged humanity as political expediency. Although no delay took place in the decision to send this expedition and in the completion of the arrangements for its despatch, it was not till December 1756 that Clive and the squadron under Admiral Watson, his comrade in arms against Angria, arrived in the Hughli. The interval had given Surajah confidence, but it had also caused him to realise that by suppressing the English factory he had lost a promising source of revenue. He had no fear of retribution at the hands of the English, but he was disposed to restore Calcutta, still in the possession of his garrison, and to grant fresh trade facilities. Such were his feelings when news reached him that Clive had entered the river, recovered Fort William, and destroyed his garrison at Hughli. He was still anxious for an amicable settlement and proposed to compensate the members of the Calcutta factory for their losses and sufferings. These Englishmen themselves were willing to meet him half way. They had run away from Calcutta in the first place, and thought nothing of glory or of political expansion. They wanted their money bags replenished out of the Mogul treasury and to resume their ordinary pursuits. But Clive took a very different view of the situation, and although hampered by the Calcutta Board and also by the Madras Council—who wanted him back to fight the French—he succeeded in carrying out his own policy.

The conduct of Surajah Dowlah himself no doubt largely contributed to Clive's success. That Prince took military steps which were incompatible with his peaceful protestations, and his agent Omichund played a double part. Clive saw the possible perils of the situation when Surajah Dowlah began to intrigue with the French, and he determined on a bold counter-stroke. War had not then been declared between England and France, but it was known to be inevitable, and Clive came to the resolution to nip in the bud all danger in Bengal from French hostility by conquering their settlement at Chandernagore. The expedition was secretly fitted out and admirably led. The French were too surprised and taken too completely at a disadvantage to offer much resistance, and the 500 French soldiers who might have turned Plassy into a Mogul victory were disarmed and made prisoners of war. At this juncture several of Surajah Dowlah's principal relatives and officers, disgusted by his treatment or disappointed by his want of success, began to plot for his overthrow. Into these intrigues Clive threw himself with energy, for he quickly saw that they provided him with the means of thwarting the pusillanimous counsels of Bengal and at the same time of turning a deaf ear to the messages of recall from Madras. Mir Jaffir, the commander of the troops, was the leader of the plot; and on its success he was promised the succession to Surajah Dowlah.

At the moment when the plot was ripe for fulfilment Omichund turned traitor, or rather he demanded the enormous sum of £300,000 as the price of his keeping faith. Clive, brought face to face with a peril that threatened the success of the whole design, resorted to villany to catch a villain. He expressed his readiness to comply with the Hindu's request. An agreement was drawn up, but Clive had two copies prepared, one on red paper, the other on white. The former contained the promise to Omichund, but was fictitious and bore the forged signature of Admiral Watson, which Clive did not scruple to append himself. The white treaty was the genuine one, and was only produced when the Hindu asked to be paid and discovered that he was to get nothing. It is unnecessary here to go into the moral side of this unpleasant matter. Clive vindicated himself some time afterwards by declaring in a letter still in existence that "delay and chicanery is allowable against those who take advantages of the times, our distresses and situations."

Having completed these preliminaries Clive gave the signal by assuming the offensive and marching towards Moorshedabad at the head of 3,000 men who, as he said, never turned their backs. Surajah Dowlah collected all his forces to repel the English, and Mir Jaffir, his courage failing him at the last moment, held back and did not join Clive with his followers as had been arranged. In this grave position, when the two forces were only separated by the plain of Plassy, Clive called a council of war, and although Eyre Coote was in favour of attack, the majority decided for retreat. Clive seemed to yield to the majority, and for an hour the fate of the English in Bengal hung in the balance. Clive then came to the momentous decision to resume his advance and to attack the Nabob's army of nearly 60,000 men with the 1,000 British and 2,000 native troops under his orders. The battle, which was fought on 23rd June 1757, was short, sharp, and decisive. The Bengal army was put to the rout one hour after the first cannon shot, and, although it lost only 500 killed, its camp, guns and baggage formed the prize of the victors. Mir Jaffir came into Clive's camp to congratulate him, not without doubt as to his reception, but his fears vanished when Clive greeted him as ruler of Bengal and its dependent provinces. Some days later the English commander installed him in the seat of Surajah Dowlah at the provincial capital of Moorshedabad. The new ruler's position was assured by the capture and murder of Surajah Dowlah.

The territorial reward to the East India Company for the victory of Plassy was not much. For the chief part of its possessions south of Calcutta it paid a rent to Mir Jaffir. The pecuniary reward was a sum of £800,000 out of the Bengal Treasury, but the most important result was the establishment in the north of the same military power and reputation which the English had acquired in the south. Having made this striking commencement Clive hastened to ensure and extend the authority and the influence of his country. He dispatched one expedition under the command of Major Forde into the region which is termed the Northern Circars; and when Shah Alum the son of the Great Mogul advanced against Mir Jaffir at the head of a large force, boasting that he would reconquer Bengal, Clive went himself to encounter the new danger. At that moment Shah Alum was closely besieging Patna, which seemed on the point of falling, but such was the terror of Clive that on hearing of his rapid approach the Mogul force broke up their camp and dispersed in all directions. In his gratitude for this rescue Mir Jaffir assigned to Clive the rent paid him by the Company for the districts mentioned, namely the 24 Pergunnahs.

At this juncture Clive was called upon to face a new and unexpected peril which threatened to destroy all that had been done.

The appearance of Lally had compelled him to send Eyre Coote and the larger portion of his European troops to Madras, and as the French power in Bengal had been destroyed there seemed no special risk in this step. But Mir Jaffir, fearful lest the power that had set him up might destroy him, had been intriguing with the Dutch at Chinsura, and the Dutch were induced to believe that by a bold stroke they might obtain on the Ganges the monopoly they had acquired in the Eastern Archipelago. They wrote to Batavia a full account of the position in Bengal, and the Dutch Governor of the Indies sent a powerful squadron and a land force of 1,500 good troops to snatch the prize Providence seemed to have placed within his reach. He reckoned without Clive, and he presumed too much on the nominal peace between Holland and England deterring the English from attacking an armed expedition directed against themselves. Such considerations had not prevented the Dutch murdering Englishmen at Amboyna, they did not weigh a feather with Clive when he saw that he had to preserve the British possessions in Bengal. To reach Chinsura the Dutch had to sail up the Hughli and past Calcutta. Clive at the head of a very inferior naval and military force met them on the way, attacked and defeated them, destroyed several of their largest ships, and imposed on the Dutch of Chinsura the onerous condition that they were never to interfere in politics again as the price of their retention of that factory. It was immediately after this extraordinary success that Clive returned for a second time to England.

After his departure Mir Jaffir was deposed by the British, and Mir Casim was set up in his place. But Mir Casim also turned on the English, and having perpetrated a massacre of 200 English prisoners at Patna fled before an avenging force under Major Munro into Oude. The Nawab Wazir of that state, and Shah Alum, who had now become the Great Mogul, took up his cause, and the confederated princes placed in the field the most formidable native army that had yet been gathered in Northern India. On the 23rd October 1764, it met and was signally defeated by the Anglo-Indian army under Major Munro at Buxar. That battle was in its way as decisive and striking as Plassy. It placed Oude at our mercy, and the Mogul Emperor visited the English camp as a suppliant. It was at first proposed to retain Oude, but during the negotiations Clive arrived a third time from England and he restored it to the Nawab Wazir, taking instead from the Emperor the divisions of Bengal, Behar, and Orissa. To these were added in the next year by treaty with the Nizam the

Northern Circars. With these acquisitions England first became a territorial power in Bengal. In the seven years from Plassy to Buxar the military position in Bengal was placed on so indisputable a basis that it passed without challenge in that vast province from the day of Munro's victory to the Mutiny.

Not long after Clive's final departure from Calcutta in January 1767 a crisis arose in Southern India which threatened to prove more difficult to deal with than the rivalry of French governors and adventurers. In the productive and interesting kingdom of Mysore the native Hindu dynasty, which had maintained its independence long after the Mogul advance south of the Nerbudda, had been lately set aside by a Mahomedan soldier of fortune named Hyder Ali. Before Dupleix fell or Clive established his military reputation Hyder Ali had begun the career which made him the most striking Indian figure of the eighteenth century and our most formidable adversary. When Munro won Buxar he had become the sovereign of Mysore and a potentate with whom his neighbours must reckon. It was not till the end of the year 1767 that he crossed the path of the English, and then only because the Nizam of the Deccan regretting the loss of the Circars resolved for the first and last time to array his forces against the English. Bussy took a considerable part in organising the compaign, but treachery was the main weapon relied on. The Nizam's force was defeated at Vellore, and the worst peril from the confederacy seemed passed when Hyder Ali descending from his mountain kingdom at the head of 30,000 men plundered the Carnatic and compelled the English authorities at Madras to purchase an ignominious peace by concluding an alliance with him. For ten years after this incident Hyder Ali's power seemed greater than that of the English in Madras.

During that period the affairs of the Company were guided by little men, but in 1774 Warren Hastings, appointed the first Governor-General of Bengal, resumed the execution of the task that Clive had first begun. The military exploits of Clive might never have borne the fruit they did if at so short an interval the statesmanship and administrative skill of Warren Hastings had not supervened for their consolidation. Warren Hastings reformed the European administration, but his chief achievements were the repudiation of the Mogul's authority by refusing to pay the tribute of 300,000 rs. a year, the seizure of Allahabad, and the increase of the Company's revenue from these and similar high-handed and unjustifiable causes. From the moral point of view there is nothing to be said for them. They were the acts of a conqueror, and made the more remarkable because effected without the least employment of force. In this manner Hastings added a quarter of a million to the Company's revenue, and obtained a capital sum of half a million, which was doubled by the subjugation of the Rohillas for the benefit of the ruler of Oude. These funds provided Hastings with the means of carrying on the important and serious wars that marked the later years of his administration. Without those funds he could not have brought them to a triumphant issue.

The first opponents with whom Hastings felt it necessary to deal were the Marathas, who under the titular head of Sivaji's successor, the Rajah of Sattara, had founded the then great military states of Baroda, Gwalior and Indore. It was said that France, baffled in the south, had sent emissaries to these Courts to stir them up against the English, and the authorities in Bombay were filled with alarm as to whether they could hold their own. Hastings at once realised the gravity of the position ; he raised ten new native regiments, and he sent two expeditions across India to Bombay. Captain Popham stormed Scindiah's reputedly impregnable fort of Gwalior, Colonel Goddard overthrew the Gaikwar of Baroda, and the danger was dispelled. A peace on lenient terms was granted to the Marathas, for in the south a more ominous cloud had arisen. Hyder Ali, with the co-operation of Bussy, invaded Madras in 1780, but the diplomacy of Hastings had fortunately succeeded in detaching the Nizam from his side, and although one English brigade, under Baillie, was cut up, and the chief commander, Sir Hector Munro, was compelled to retreat, nothing irretrievable occurred before the arrival of Sir Eyre Coote, who vindicated the military honour of his country, as already described, at Porto Novo. The war lingered on until after the death of Hyder Ali in 1782, but the danger to Madras was finally staved off, and Bussy's scheme for the overthrow of the English shared the same fate as Lally's.

While this arduous campaign was in progress in the south Hastings achieved easier and more profitable triumphs in the north. The Rajah of Benares incurred his anger and felt his heavy hand, and the holy city of the Hindus passed under the control of the English, who were now steadily pushing their way up the Ganges to the limits of the Emperor's own personal authority. The Nawab of Oude and the Begums or Princesses of Oude were compelled to disgorge large sums for the benefit of the Company, and the only thing that can be said in extenuation of these measures of extortion is that without them Hastings could not have maintained his position, and the many enemies of the English would eventually have triumphed not by their martial qualities but by their superior resources. Warren Hastings overcame two grave perils in Madras and the Maratha country, but his chief contribution to the making of India was the discovery of the sources of revenue which enabled the Company to play its new political and imperial part.

Hastings was succeeded after a brief interregnum by Earl (afterwards Marquis) Cornwallis, an appointment chiefly interesting because it testified to the increasing importance of an office hitherto monopolised by one of the Company's servants. His tenure of power was chiefly remarkable for the first war with Tippoo Sahib, son and successor of Hyder Ali. The war began at the end of 1789 with Tippoo's attack on Travancore, and the greatness of the danger in the eyes of the English authorities can be inferred from the fact that Cornwallis exerted all the influence of the Government to conclude an alliance with the Nizam and the Marathas against the ruler of Mysore. The negotiations were successful, and at the least this signified the isolation of Tippoo, which became more complete as Britain recovered the mastery of the seas which had been temporarily lost in the time of Suffren. Lord Cornwallis took the command of the army in person, and during the whole of the year 1791 Southern

India was the scene of a bitter and stubborn contest, which did not close until the haughty "tiger of Seringapatam" was beleaguered in his capital. Then he agreed to surrender half his territory, to pay three millions sterling and to give his sons as hostages.

But the settlement of this question was not reached in the time of Lord Cornwallis. His successor, Sir John Shore, was a man of peace; but in 1798 the Marquis Wellesley arrived in India specially charged with the mission of establishing British predominance in the peninsula, and filled with Pitt's convictions that the fate of the world depended on the life and death struggle between England and France. At that moment with Bonaparte in Egypt every vestige of French power in India became or magnified importance. The Nizam's army had been trained by Bussy and other French officers, Scindiah's army was becoming really formidable in the hands of De Boigne, and Tippoo's sympathies were French. Wellesley went to work at once. He cajoled or frightened the Nizam into dismissing his French officers, disbanding his regiments, and signing a treaty promising to employ no Europeans except Englishmen. Having made himself secure at Hyderabad he declared war on Tippoo, invaded his state with two armies, and captured his capital by assault. Tippoo himself was slain in the breach, and from that date, the 4th of

May 1799, Southern India has been tranquil. No danger has arisen or seems capable of arising in that quarter of the peninsula where the foundation of our power was first laid.

A more serious task awaited Lord Wellesley than the overthrow of the system of Tippoo, already shaken by the previous campaigns with Lord Cornwallis. He endeavoured to make the Maratha chiefs accept an arrangement similar to that he had imposed on the Nizam, and when he exacted from the Peishwa the Treaty of Bassein embodying such an arrangement it seemed as if his end might be attained by peaceful means. But the militant chiefs repudiated the action of the Peishwa who had been expelled from his capital by Holkar, and Scindiah and the Rajah of Nagpur formed a defensive and offensive alliance to resist the pretensions of the English. It was in this emergency that Wellesley showed the highest gifts of statesmanship, and he was fortunate enough to find in his younger brother, the future Duke of Wellington, and General Lake two extremely able commanders to realise his schemes. The campaigns which followed were among the most brilliant and successful in the whole of our Eastern experience. Sir Arthur Wellesley won the battles of Assaye and Argaum, and captured the strong fortress of Ahmednugger. Lake gained still more striking victories at Aligarh and Laswari and concluded a most remarkable march at Delhi with the rescue of the Mogul Emperor from his Maratha gaolers. The reader must not imagine that these battles were won with ease or without loss. The Marathas fought with the greatest courage; they were only vanquished by superior skill and exceptional military genius. The result of these wars was that the two largest and best trained Maratha armies were vanquished and humiliated, that large provinces were annexed to the territories of the Company and its allies, and that the Mogul Emperor passed from the tutelage of the Marathas to that of the English.

A second struggle began with Holkar, but the want of funds added to the dissatisfaction of the Company at the cost of the war compelled Wellesley to make peace before any decisive result was attained. Holkar's territory was somewhat diminished, but at the moment of the termination of hostilities he showed his defiance by concluding an alliance with his hereditary enemy Scindiah. Peace was however preserved for several years, as the next Governor-Generals were peaceful and prevented by their orders from embarking on military adventures. Even Lord Minto, a statesman of broad views, was only allowed to crush the French in the Mauritius and Java and by these successes to finally preclude European influences from making themselves felt within the peninsula.

The Governor-Generalship of Lord Hastings, which began in 1813 and lasted till 1823, was among the most important epochs in Anglo-Indian history and may be compared with those of Warren Hastings, Wellesley, and in later times Dalhousie. It might have proved more epoch-making than it did but for a stubborn campaign which had to be fought soon after its commencement with the gallant Goorkha tribes of Nepaul. There we learnt first to respect and value the martial qualities of a race which has ever since ranked among our most loyal and distinguished auxiliaries. The year 1817 began with a war against the Pindari bands which held the whole of Central India and with whom the greater Maratha chiefs were more or less in sympathy and alliance. No sooner had Lord Hastings succeeded in overcoming this danger than he was confronted by another and graver one in the alliance of Holkar and Nagpur supported by all the weight of the Peishwa's name. Fortunately Scindiah stood aloof in the second Maratha war, which was brought to a speedy and successful conclusion by the signal defeat at Mehidpore of Holkar's army. After this desperate struggle and conclusive triumph which concluded our twenty years' contest with the Marathas a long internal peace followed in India. With the exception of the first Burmese war in 1826 and the capture in the same year of the strong fortress of Bhurtpore, which was not retained, there was peace throughout the peninsula until the Afghan campaign of 1839.

The conquest of India, which practically began with the battle of Plassy in 1757, may be considered completed by the second Maratha war in 1817. In sixty years the East India Company had extended its dominion from the few factories and trading ports stationed around the coast over the whole of the peninsula outside the Punjab. The Viceroys of the Mogul in Bengal, the Deccan and Oude had been either superseded or reduced to a position of subordination. The most formidable military races, the Mahomedans of Mysore, the Marathas of every principality from Delhi to the Nerbudda, and the Rohilla Afghans of Northern India, had in turn been compelled to yield to the steady discipline and unsurpassable courage of the English. Kings held their states at the pleasure of that trading Company whose origin had been humble, whose fortunes had long been checkered by reverses, and whose greatness had been thrust upon it. The great Mogul, whose Imperial power seemed so irresistible at the beginning of the seventeenth century, had become in the early years of the nineteenth the puppet of the English, thankful that their protection was less irksome and less costly than that of the Marathas,

CHAPTER VI.

THE DECLINE AND FALL OF THE COMPANY.

ALTHOUGH the decline of the East India Company is generally dated from the expedition into Afghanistan, and may to some extent have been hastened by the untoward incidents of that campaign, the evidence of military power continued to be displayed up to the very hour of the Mutiny in such a manner as seemed to dispel all idea of danger or decay. Before briefly describing the salient features of the first Afghan War, it will be useful to note some changes of importance that had been made in the constitution of the Company, and in its prerogatives. Originally the Company had been independent of all control and possessed a monopoly of the trade with India and China. The servants of the Company were allowed to trade on their own account and to take presents from the native chiefs. When Clive was sent out on the third occasion he put down this system, and in the time of Warren Hastings the servants of the Company received a fixed pay followed by a pension, of which latter fund Mir Jaffir's jaghir to Clive formed by his voluntary surrender the nucleus. In 1773 the Regulating Act more clearly defined the position of the Company and sanctioned the elevation of its head authority into a Governor-General. In 1783 Pitt's India Act established the Board of Control, an office in London for the supervision of the policy and administration of the Company in India. In return for submitting to that restraint the Charter was prolonged for thirty years, but when its renewal was granted in 1813 the monopoly of Indian trade was shorn from it and a loud cry of ruin was raised by the proprietors. In 1833 the monopoly of the China trade was also taken from it, so that in this year the commercial functions of the East India Company, which had been gradually diminishing, finally disappeared.

During the same period a number of reforms in the administration had been carried out, and Lord William Bentinck—the first to bear the full title of Governor-General of India—will always rank foremost among the benefactors of the Hindu races. If his name is chiefly associated with the abolition of Suttee—the compulsory immolation of Hindu widows on their husbands' biers—he conferred equally signal benefits on the people by his patronage of education, by the admission of natives into the civil service, and by making the roads secure for travellers, the "thugs" or professional poisoners who frequented them being hunted down. It was he who decreed that English should be the universal official language of the peninsula and that the Press should be absolutely free, although these laws did not come into effect until the time of his successor Lord Metcalfe. Evidence was thus afforded that the English were not mere conquerors or mere traders. In the time of Lord William Bentinck they first stood forth as the benefactors of the human race, and their reputation for justice reached perhaps a higher point than it has ever attained since. In the whole range of Anglo-Indian episodes there is not one more effective or more characteristic than that of Sir Charles Metcalfe taking the young Maharajah of Jeypore, one of the chief Rajput princes, on his knee in the midst of an angry and excited durbar, and proclaiming that the English Raj had taken him under its protection. Great was the power of the Sirkar or Government in those days! Its armies had never known defeat, its sway was beneficent, and it held forth to the millions of the peninsula a higher standard of justice, security and nobleness than any of its predecessors had approached.

The fear of France had been a potent force in our Indian politics for half a century: in the time of Lord William Bentinck it was superseded or rather replaced by a corresponding dread of Russia, which has operated ever since as a vital influence permanently affecting the bent of our external policy in India. That statesman and soldier drew up an important State paper showing how a Russian army might invade India, and several adventurous travellers—of whom Burnes and Arthur Conolly deserve special mention—brought back from Central Asia news of Russian movements and ambition. No overt step was taken until the year 1838, Lord Auckland being Governor-General, when an unreasoning fear of Russia and an over-confident view of our own position impelled us to interfere in the internal affairs of Afghanistan with the idea of setting up a friendly potentate on the throne of Cabul. The occupant of that position, a man of great ability named Dost Mahomed, grandfather of the present Ameer, was said to have been won over by a Russian envoy, and it was decided to take up the cause of Shah Shujah, then an exile in India but the chief representative of the royal family of Afghanistan. With this view an alliance was concluded with Runjeet Singh, the Sikh ruler of the Punjab, and in January 1839 the Anglo-Indian army crossed the Indus at Sukhur and began its march on Candahar. The campaign that followed was most brilliant, and considering that Lord Keane's force was mainly composed of the old Hindustani Sepoys armed with the old Brown Bess musket—a weapon inferior in several respects to the Afghan jezail—there has never been a war in Asia on which we might with greater reason pride ourselves than this first campaign in Afghanistan. In little more than three months our army captured Candahar, stormed the reputedly impregnable fortress of Ghuzni, and occupied the capital, Cabul, after having vanquished the principal national army in the open field. Shah Shujah was placed on the throne, and if our army had only been withdrawn as promptly as it had advanced all would have been well. Very probably Shah Shujah would have failed to maintain himself against his abler rival, but an impression would have been left west of the passes of the daring and invincibility of the new Lords of India.

But if valour led the armies of the Company reason did not sit on this occasion at her Council table. It was decided to prop up the prince whose cause we had espoused, for it was said we could not abandon our nominee, and at the same time we reduced our garrison to the lowest possible figure. In 1840 Dost Mahomed attempted to renew the struggle but he was defeated, and the greatness of the English reputation may be gathered from the fact that he voluntarily surrendered himself when he could easily have escaped. As we had no intention of annexing Afghanistan,—indeed such a project was at the moment quite impracticable owing to the British territory in India being cut off by the intermediate independent Sikh kingdom of the Punjab,—it seems incredible that this second favourable opportunity for evacuation was not seized. History has never been able to explain such acts of folly except on the theory of the inexorable decrees of Fate. Our garrison remained on, and the year 1841 became one of the blackest in our national annals. The Afghans are a brave and freedom-loving race. They have fought bravely against us and for us, and in the future as in the past they must represent an important force on the North-west borders of India. In 1841 they rose in insurrection, and when the charm of English invincibility was broken the position of the small Anglo-Indian force soon became grave and almost desperate. Where the courage of the commander remained undiminished, as was the case with General Nott at Candahar, there the enemy was not merely kept at bay but beaten whenever encountered; but at Cabul the presumption and folly of our political, and the irresolution of our military representatives entailed defeat and disgrace which culminated in the destruction of an armed brigade of 4,000 men and 12,000 unarmed followers.

This was both the first and the greatest military calamity to befall us in India. In 1842 an avenging army was sent into the country under Sir George Pollock, the Afghans were defeated in several encounters, "the illustrious garrison" of Jellalabad as it was specially called was rescued, the equally illustrious garrison of Candahar was permitted to retire in triumph from that place *viâ* Cabul, and before the close of the year 1842 there was not a British soldier left in the country. Shah Shujah had been got rid of before our military triumph was complete, and when we evacuated the country we had not even the satisfaction of leaving behind us a government of our own choice. Dost Mahomed was released from his confinement in India, and allowed to resume the authority in which a wiser policy would have kept him undisturbed.

If the Afghan war had been between equals the triumph of 1842 would have completely wiped out the failure of 1841, but no subsequent success could obliterate the fact that English troops had been vanquished in battle. For a quarter of a century no competitor had ventured to draw the sword against us in India, but those who retained the wish of supremacy now felt revived hope. The troops were scarcely back from Cabul when the smouldering fires that must always be latent in some section of Indian society burst into a flame in Gwalior, the state ruled by the house of Scindiah. The chief himself was a child and took no part in the revolt of his army. A brief but desperate campaign followed, and it was only after the Maratha army had been thoroughly beaten in two great battles at Maharajpure and Punneah that peace was restored. Had this Maratha rising been timed to coincide with the Sikh defiance two years later, there is no doubt that British power in India would have been subjected to a severe strain, but fortunately Central India was effectually tranquillised and the last of the Maratha armies was practically destroyed when the long-threatening war clouds burst on the Sutlej in 1845.

The Sikhs had been our allies in the Afghan adventure. Their chief Runjeet Singh was a signatory of the Tripartite treaty with Shah Shujah, but his death in 1839 had destroyed this good understanding. Before General Pollock's force had returned from Cabul the opinion was freely held that the Sikhs had not kept faith with us, and the Sikhs were undoubtedly husbanding their military power for some serious ordeal. The English conquest of the great province of Scinde in 1843, when Sir Charles Napier won the fierce battle of Meeanee and sent his famous laconic message *Peccavi* —or in other words "I have Scinde"—was a warning to the Sikhs, for it placed the lower course of the Indus in our hands. The warning was not heeded, for after two years threatening the army of the Sikh Khalsa which had been trained by Avitabile and other foreign adventurers crossed the Sutlej and invaded British territory. At that moment Lord Hardinge, a Peninsular and Waterloo veteran and one of Wellington's favourite lieutenants, was Governor-General, and he hastened to the front to superintend the military operations; but the actual command was held by Lord Gough, an impetuous soldier who had recently made a reputation in China by the capture of Canton. The first battle of the war was fought at Moodkee on the 18th of December 1845 and the last battle on the following 10th of February at Sobraon. Between those two actions occurred the equally severe struggles at Aliwal and Ferozeshah. These four encounters were of unexampled ferocity, but in each of them the Sikhs were decidedly beaten. When they had been driven across the Sutlej they were compelled to sign a treaty of peace at their capital, Lahore, and to surrender the Jullunder Doab, that portion of the Punjab lying between that river and the Beas.

This treaty proved only a truce, for the warlike spirit of the Sikhs was not broken, and despite the confusion prevailing in their own Government their army was ready for a second trial of strength. The second Sikh War began in 1848 with the murder of two English officers, Vans Agnew and Anderson, at Moultan, and before the end of the year Lord Gough had won several minor successes, of which the most important was achieved at Ramnugger. The principal Sikh army occupied however a strong and carefully prepared position at Chillianwallah, near the river Chenab, and there they were attacked by Lord Gough on the 13th of January 1849. The attack was made in a somewhat reckless fashion and without any preliminary artillery engagement which was the simple explanation of what followed. The English troops, although only one-third the number of the Sikhs—and it should be remembered that the bulk of our army was native—attacked with the greatest gallantry, and when night closed remained masters of the field; but the loss had been heavy, about 2,500 killed and wounded, and the confidence of the force had been rudely shaken. The next day the English general slowly retreated without molestation to dispose of his wounded and to await reinforcements.

Chillianwallah was regarded as a defeat, and in its moral effect it was one. When the news reached London there was the greatest excitement, and the Duke of Wellington exclaimed to Sir Charles Napier "You must go, or I must go." In the hurry and scare of the moment Napier was sent out as Commander-in-Chief,—an unjust reflection on the gallant Gough, the victor on so many memorable occasions,—but long before he reached India Lord Gough had redeemed his laurels by a decisive victory. A few weeks after Chillianwallah that commander marched to meet the Sikhs at the head of an army of 25,000 men. He encountered them at Guzerat on 21st February 1849, and having preceded his attack with a vigorous and destructive artillery fire gained the most signal and decisive victory. Three weeks later the remains of the Sikh army laid down their arms, the great province of the Punjab was annexed by the new Governor-General, the famous Lord Dalhousie, and the Company's territory embraced the upper part of the Indus as it had the lower and became adjacent to Afghanistan.

Lord Dalhousie's subsequent acts of conquest may be briefly enumerated. In 1852, after a second war with the foolish and unreasonable

King of Burmah, the province of Pegu with the mouths of the Irrawaddy and the important harbour of Rangoon became British. In 1853 Berar was taken from the Nizam, and in 1856 Oude, the most important Mahomedan State of India, was also annexed. In the same year an expedition to the Persian Gulf under Sir James Outram was completely successful, and the Persians who had seized the far-famed fortress of Herat were compelled to evacuate it. Amid these unusual demonstrations of our power and reputation the eventful administration of Lord Dalhousie terminated. It had been an epoch that ranked in importance with any in our Indian history, and his achievements placed him on the same list as Clive, Hastings and Wellesley. There was no indication of declining power; rather might it have been said that the invincibility of the Company had been placed beyond further possibility of demonstration, for from Cashmere to Cape Comorin there was not left a military force entitled to the name of an army. It was at that moment of seemingly indisputable triumph that the greatest danger of the century suddenly beset us, and entailed the fall of the great Company which seemed far above the assaults of adverse fortune.

The conquest of India had been effected with such rapidity and over such odds and difficulties that there was neither time nor inclination to reflect on the basis of British power in India, or on the perils that might attend the progress of empire. Still, some highly gifted persons had scanned the future with anxiety. Henry Lawrence and John Jacob, two of the most competent military leaders of their day, had independently come to the same conclusion, namely, that the native army, the force which had made the East India Company, might destroy it. These words of wisdom were written fourteen years before the blow fell. They were uttered to deaf ears, and had long been forgotten when the crisis arrived. The native or Sepoy army had necessarily been largely increased by the wars with the Marathas, the Afghans and the Sikhs, until at this period it was not far short of 350,000 men. The force was of the three arms, and the main portion of the artillery was worked by Sepoys. At the same time the European garrison rarely exceeded 25,000 men. There was consequently a very glaring disparity in numbers, and in the distribution of troops many districts were left without any English garrison. The Sepoys were not then mainly composed as at present of special warlike races, but were taken as they presented themselves from the mass of the Hindu and Mussulman races, so that they continued in close touch and sympathy with the civil population. They were consequently open to all the influences of anti-English sentiment worked upon by waves of superstition, offended popular prejudice by interference with established custom, and the ambitious schemes of a few designing men.

The native regiments were the pulse of the native races, but in their exaggerated belief in the loyalty of their men the officers refused to feel that pulse or to allow anyone else to detect the approach of fever. Yet, creditable as was the military record of the Sepoy army, it had on occasions, rare and isolated it is true, given evidence of an insubordinate spirit. In 1806 a mutiny had broken out at Vellore which led to the execution of 800 Sepoys. Three years later there had been a similar rising at Seringapatam, and in 1827 the Bengal army followed with a mutiny at Barrackpore—when the 47th Regiment was exterminated to a man on its own parade ground—the bad example set it by Madras. On the principle that what has happened once may occur again, the military authorities might well have believed in the abstract possibility of a mutiny of the native army. But there were special reasons for apprehending that the army of 1857 might prove less amenable to reason than its predecessors. It had been increased by the necessities of war to vast and unwieldy proportions, yet no one ventured to suggest that it should be reduced to a more reasonable size. The men, by the extra allowance or "batta" given during active campaigning, had grown accustomed, during wars that seemed never to cease, to a scale of pay much in excess of that paid them in cantonments; and after the annexation of the Punjab it looked as if permanent peace had settled down over the peninsula and that the sword would be turned into the scythe. The native troops also believed that they were the buttress of the Company's power, for, as has been pointed out, the European troops were few in number and represented rather the Old Guard of the Company than the recognised garrison of its territory.

It was at the moment that such thoughts were uppermost in the minds of the Sepoys that it was decided to introduce a new cartridge. There was nothing in that article to justify the dislike with which the Sepoys seemed to instinctively regard it or to support the view that its use involved a breach of caste for the Hindus, and a personal insult to the Mahomedans. But it served the purpose of the intriguers who had for some years been organising, and preparing the way for, a seditious movement. The secret history of the movement will perhaps never be known, but undoubtedly one of the chief instigators of the revolt was Nana Sahib, the adopted heir of Baji Rao, the ex-Peishwa, to whom with questionable justice and still more questionable economy we declined to continue the pension. Round him gathered the cleverest intriguers of the old Maratha court, while the Mahomedans were offended and alarmed by the summary proceedings in Oude, the home of a large portion of the Bengal army. It was their emissaries, no doubt, who sent the mysterious chupatties—cakes bearing a silent and secret message—who denounced the cartridges, and who disseminated the superstitious prophecy that Heaven had decreed the fall of the Company on the centenary of Plassy.

If the Sepoys had not been ripe for revolt for their own special reasons, some of which have been glanced at, it is very possible that the machinations of ambitious and disappointed intriguers would have borne no fruit; but a concatenation of circumstances, of which not the least was the extraordinary and delusive confidence in which the English themselves were lulled, contributed to the spread and success of a movement that a watchful or even a suspicious Government would have strangled at its birth. On the 24th of January 1857 the first open mutiny occurred at Berhampore, and a native regiment was sent from that place to Barrackpore, the chief cantonment near

Calcutta, to be disbanded. A second regiment followed its example and shared its fate. Early in May a third regiment mutinied at Lucknow, and was disarmed by Sir Henry Lawrence. On the 10th of May the native troops at the important station of Meerut mutinied, killed some of their officers, fired the lines and made their escape to Delhi. The capture of that important city and of the Emperor, who still retained the title of the Great Mogul, although all vestige of his power had long disappeared, gave the mutineers a political importance they had not possessed up to that moment. The significance of the capture of Delhi would have been far greater if the rebels had secured the Arsenal, but the heroism of two English officers, by a deed of self-immolation that has never been surpassed, baffled the foe by exploding the contents of the building.

After the seizure of Delhi there was a lull of three weeks, and it was not until the end of May that the four Sepoy regiments at Lucknow turned their muskets on their officers, or for another month that Sir Henry Lawrence felt compelled to retire into the Residency, which with infinite resource he had placed in a position to stand a siege. A few days before, Cawnpore—the base of Lucknow on the Ganges—had witnessed the surrender of the English garrison to Nana Sahib, who with oriental duplicity massacred his prisoners including the women and children after he had promised them their lives. This savage and treacherous act imparted a ferocity into the struggle that would otherwise have been absent, and the Well of Cawnpore remains as a standing warning against over-confidence in India. By this time the whole of Northern India, with the exception of the Punjab, was ablaze with mutiny and rebellion. The whole of the Bengal army had thrown off its allegiance, and in Central India the Maratha armies of Holkar and Scindiah showed that they too could not be held back by the influence of their chiefs. But the two principal centres of danger were at Delhi and Lucknow. The possession of the former place gave the rebels a power they would not otherwise have acquired, and at the latter a small band of Englishmen were holding out in a feeble position against overwhelming odds. Space will not admit of the baldest description of the Titanic struggle that ensued, but in the sea of difficulties by which our countrymen were beset in the early summer of 1857 recognition must be made of two circumstances which in the most providential manner contributed to enable them to hold their own until succour came across the seas from England. These were the loyalty of the Sikhs and the passage across the Indian Ocean of an English expedition on its way to China.

The struggle with the Sikhs and the annexation of the province of the Punjab have been described. The Sikhs fought us bravely and unflinchingly. Not eight years had elapsed from Chillianwallah, when the signal went forth that the Sirkar was doomed, and the wounds of that struggle might still have been deemed fresh. But the Sikhs were a noble race, and bore their recent adversaries no rancour. They respected courage, and let it ever be remembered to their credit they refused to take advantage of our troubles, or to turn on us in our adversity, or to play the game of other races whom they despised. Although many great Englishmen—Henry Lawrence, John Nicholson and Herbert Edwardes pre-eminent among them—had laboured, and not in vain, to win their confidence, the loyalty and staunchness of the Sikhs to our side was not a thing on which we had any reason to count in 1857. I am not going, in imitation of a prevalent bad practice of attributing to a single cause the result of many combined circumstances, to the extreme of saying that the Sikhs saved British India, but it would be ungrateful if we ever forgot or seemed to disparage the touching devotion of a race which gave its blood freely on our side in the supreme crisis of our Indian career.

The English troops arrested at Singapore on their way to China provided the garrison which secured Lower Bengal, and the column placed under the command of Sir Henry Havelock for the relief of the hard-pressed garrison of the Lucknow Residency. Although this column never exceeded 3,000 men Havelock fought his way to Cawnpore, inflicting several defeats on the mutineers and entering the town the day after the massacre. A few days later he defeated the main army of Nana Sahib at Bithoor. He was not in a position to relieve Lucknow until the end of September, and in connection with that splendid exploit the chivalrous conduct of his comrade in arms Sir James Outram deserves to be signalised. Outram had been appointed to the command as the senior officer over Havelock's head at a moment when Havelock had done much towards completing his plan of rescue, but Outram refused to deprive him of the command and served as a volunteer on his staff until after the relief of the Residency. Such chivalrous actions well entitled Outram to his name as the Bayard of India. The relief of the Residency on the 25th of September 1857 was very far from closing the operations at Lucknow. The reinforced garrison took up a new position while Colin Campbell, Lord Clyde, the new Commander-in-Chief, made his arrangements for the final overthrow of the rebel forces, which had collected in the large city of Lucknow to the extent it is said of 100,000 armed men, the majority of whom had been our own trained Sepoys. On the 21st of March 1858 the enemy was driven out of Lucknow after a series of Homeric struggles, during one of which 2,000 mutineers were bayoneted in a Palace from which retreat was impossible.

Four days before the relief of the Residency, Delhi, the Imperial city, had been recovered by assault. During its siege the same qualities of fortitude in the face of difficulty and of scorn for superior numbers had been evinced by the handful of British, Sikh and Goorkha soldiery on the Ridge. If Henry Lawrence, killed unfortunately in the first days of the defence, but whose spirit animated the garrison to the last, was the hero of the Residency, and Havelock of the relief, John Nicholson was the soul of the siege and assault of Delhi. To his spirit and dauntless courage its capture was largely due, but his death dimmed the satisfaction of victory. By the end of 1857 large reinforcements had arrived from England. Two armies were directed to march through Central India, and one of them under Sir Hugh Rose—afterwards Lord Strathnairn—carried out a campaign remarkable for its celerity and success. It ranks by general consent with Havelock's capture of Cawnpore and relief of Lucknow as the two finest feats of the whole struggle in the larger measures of war. Of the smaller acts it is impossible to speak, yet a passing tribute may be paid to the loyalty of Salar Jung the Hyderabad statesman, and of Jung Bahadur of Nepaul.

The Mutiny sealed the fate of the great Company which had represented this country in the East for a century. The opinion had long been held that India was too important and weighty a charge to be held by a private association. No one could justly blame the Company for the Mutiny, yet it obviously marked an appropriate termination for the old state of things and a suitable starting point for a new. On the 1st of September 1858 the announcement was made of the termination of the East India Company's rule, and two months later the direct sovereignty of the Queen was proclaimed, Lord Canning the Governor-General of the Mutiny assuming at the same date the style of Viceroy. The reader who has followed in this brief chronicle the humble origin, the slow growth, and the magnificent development of the East India Company will not think that it needs any monument or testimonial. Its achievements speak for themselves. They form a considerable and glorious part of the greatness of England.

CHAPTER VII.

THE INDIA OF THE QUEEN.

IF it were asked what is the principal difference between the India of the Queen and the India of the Company, the unanimous answer of all authorities would be that, whereas the Company never ceased to annex the territories of the native princes of the peninsula and displayed an ambition to the very last hour of its life to absorb the whole of the country within its own administration, the Queen has not annexed a yard of territory within the frontier, and she has even given back one important state to its native dynasty. In this the Queen has been true to her word as conveyed in the Royal Proclamation on assuming the sovereignty of India, for therein occurs the guarantee of their possessions to the Princes on the one condition of good government. This promise, given spontaneously at a moment when angry feelings were paramount, tranquillised Indian opinion, while its exact fulfilment during forty years has mainly contributed to that growth of loyal feeling towards the Throne on the part of the Indian feudatories which has been one of the marked features of the Victorian epoch. Although the Indian ruling Princes remained loyal throughout the Mutiny, several of their armies mutinied and fought against us. It would have been in accordance with precedent if the Princes had been treated by the light of the acts of their subjects and not by their own attitude, but a juster way of looking at things came into vogue with the Queen's assumption of power, and with it confidence and a new sense of security spread through every court and capital of India. There have indeed been one or two changes in the person of a ruler of a native state—the most notable case being that of the Gaikwar who was alleged to have poisoned the British Resident—for misgovernment, but in every case authority was continued in the same ruling family, and the great principality of Mysore was restored to its hereditary Maharajah in 1881 after 50 years of British occupation.

But if the period of the Queen's rule has been remarkable for internal tranquillity it cannot be described as peaceful beyond the frontier. Yet we must admit that those external complications and campaigns have contributed a good deal to the unification of Indian sentiment under the ægis of the British sovereign. They have at least evoked loud expressions of loyal and, let it be added, patriotic feeling; they have given the Princes a definite place in the defence of India, and they have provided them with an object in which they can take a hearty and traditional interest, for until the institution of the Imperial Service Corps the hereditary military career was dead for the noblest races of the peninsula.

The annexation of the Punjab in 1849 had brought us into contact with Afghanistan, and two treaties concluded in the next seven years—coupled with our recovery of Herat by the war with Persia—had done something to place our relations with that state on a satisfactory footing. They served at least to keep the old Ameer Dost Mahomed inactive during the Mutiny. But that annexation had also brought us up to the possessions of lawless, predatory, and warlike tribes, whose hand was against everyone and who held the range of mountains that forms the western boundary of India. This region was correctly described as a "No man's land," for within it the writ of neither the Ameer nor the Queen ran. The establishment of a regular authority over the border districts was irksome to them because it put a stop to the raids they had been in the habit of executing on the cultivated districts and especially in the Peshawur valley. Then began a warfare which has been carried on with scarcely any intermission ever since and which even at the present hour cannot be called closed. But the first and most serious campaign of this character was largely influenced by political motives. A band of Hindustani fanatics, who had escaped from pursuit after the Mutiny, established a colony in the hills round Umbeyla beyond our frontier. There they stirred up some of the Pathan tribes, and their numbers increased to such large proportions that it was deemed advisable to take active measures against them before they had consolidated their position or banded further tribes in a league against us. In 1863 a considerable expedition was fitted out against them, and after the true difficulties became revealed it was increased to the size of an army. The fighting that ensued was of a most desperate character, and the Umbeyla or Black Mountain campaign was certainly the most severe and critical border war in which we were ever engaged. Similar although less grave complications have constantly recurred down to the present hour. The recent surprise of a detachment in the Tochi valley by the Waziri tribe, the rising in the Swat valley and the Afridi raids in the Khyber Pass show that a durable arrangement with these warrior tribes on a peaceful basis is still remote.

The exigencies of the Imperial position in India received a wider illustration in 1878, when we were forced into a war with the ruler of Afghanistan. That contest can only be rightly judged by a careful consideration of the events which led up to it, and space obviously renders that impossible. Afghanistan is important to the rulers of India because in the hands of an enemy it would constitute a great natural fortified camp out of which he might issue at his convenience to attack or invade India, while any attempt to expel him would be extremely hazardous. There is the old tradition to this effect crystallised into a proverb that "the lord of Delhi is not safe unless he is also master of Cabul," and there is the unimpeachable historical fact that every army issuing from Afghanistan has been victorious and every army entering it from the side of India defeated until we broke the rule in 1839 and 1842 and again in 1878 and 1879. Yet notwithstanding these well-known facts our attitude towards Afghanistan and its ruler from 1842 to 1877 was one of indifference. But we were not even consistently indifferent. During the six years of dynastic warfare that followed the death of Dost Mahomed in 1863, Lord Lawrence supported each claimant as he happened to gain some military success, and with much *naiveté* expected them all to be our friends. He exposed the vacillation of our policy by not calmly awaiting the final triumph of one prince or the other, and it so happened that the victor was the chief who had received least help from us and conceived himself most hurt by our help to others. This chief was Shere Ali, who visited India in the time of the popular Earl of Mayo, and was undoubtedly drawn towards us by that statesman. But unfortunately the impression he produced was destroyed under the next Viceroy by unwise interference with his own administration, and when Lord Lytton arrived in India with instructions to place our relations on a better footing Shere Ali had been permanently alienated.

But the true cause of our action lay outside Afghanistan. Russia had seized Khiva, and in disregard of her promise had retained its province on the right bank of the Oxus. She had also occupied Khokand and was commencing operations against the Turcomans. These facts explain the necessity felt for a clear understanding with the Ameer. Negotiations were commenced for a visit of the Ameer to India or for the despatch of a British envoy to Cabul, but they did not progress satisfactorily. It was at this moment that news was received of the arrival and reception of a

Russian general as ambassador at Cabul, and at once an English officer of high rank and reputation, Sir Neville Chamberlaine, was despatched as special envoy to the Afghan capital. On reaching the Khyber Pass he was turned back by the Afghan commandant, and an affront was thus offered the Government to which, in the East at least, it could not submit. The decision to resent it was strengthened by the knowledge that Russian intrigues had been in progress for some time in Afghanistan and that several columns of Russian troops were actually on the march for the frontier.

Three armies were directed to advance into Afghanistan at the beginning of the winter of 1878-9, and notwithstanding the lateness of the season decisive successes were obtained by each of them. The Peshawur force under Sir Samuel Browne forced the Khyber, the Kohat under General Roberts stormed the Peiwar Kotal, and the Bombay Division under Sir Donald Stewart captured Candahar. This remarkable military success paved the way for an early peace, and as Shere Ali died the task of negotiation was simplified and a definite treaty was signed with his successor Yakoob Khan. The retreat of the Russian columns referred to, through the breakdown of their commissariat arrangements, also contributed more largely than is supposed to the termination of the war. The principal clause of the treaty was the reception and residence at Cabul of an English officer with a suitable staff and escort, and Sir Louis Cavagnari, an able official long acquainted with the frontier who had acted as British Plenipotentiary, was sent to fill the perilous office of resident at the Afghan capital. He had not been there two months when the horrible news reached India that he and all his comrades, British and Indian, with the exception of a few grass-cutters, had been massacred by some of the Ameer's troops and the townspeople. This terrible event revived the memories of 1841-42, but without a trace of hesitation the Government of India ordered the necessary military steps to punish this act of hostility and perfidy on the part of the Afghans. The arrangements for evacuating Candahar had fortunately not been completed, and it was retained, while General Roberts, who had done so well in the first campaign, was entrusted with the command of the army that marched on Cabul. It will suffice here to say that the excellence of his arrangements, the celerity of his advance, and the tactical skill he displayed in the battle of Charasia, established the reputation he had already won. Cabul was occupied, the Ameer Yakoob was sent to India, and a strong and carefully prepared position at Sherpur was occupied during the winter. There was no repetition of the blunders of 1841, and when the tribes gathered and attacked our position they received a warm reception and were beaten off.

Once again in Afghanistan it was shown that our policy was not equal to our military prowess, and our difficulties were increased by there being no member of the ruling family available to put on the throne at this moment. Abdurrahman, a nephew of Shere Ali, returned from Russian Turkestan, where he had lived in exile for eleven years, and it was decided to acknowledge him as Ameer. The choice seemed a dubious one, when an event happened that showed it to be the only possible course, and that also contributed indirectly to its success. The preparations for evacuating the country were almost completed when the startling news arrived that a British regiment had been annihilated at Maiwand, a place west of Candahar, by an Afghan army that had silently moved eastwards from Herat under the command of Ayoob Khan, the younger brother of the Ameer Yakoob. On the receipt of this disastrous news it was determined to continue the withdrawal from the country, but at the same time to move a body of 10,000 specially selected troops from Cabul to Candahar with the object of retrieving as speedily as possible the reverse our arms had experienced. The command of that force was entrusted to General Roberts, who within one month of the receipt of the news of Maiwand amply avenged outside Candahar that defeat by the rout of Ayoob's army. By the same stroke we established our own position and that of our ally Abdurrahman, for there can be no doubt that if Ayoob had deferred his advance until we had withdrawn he would have swept Abdurrahman out of the country. When he renewed his attempt in 1881 with weakened force and diminished credit he almost succeeded in expelling his rival. This march to Candahar was a perfect piece of military workmanship, and established General Roberts' reputation as an able commander.

Our relations with Afghanistan, far from closing with the war, continued on a footing of closer intimacy, and in 1883 we agreed to pay the Ameer a fixed annual subsidy. By the aid of this money he has established a vigorous administration, and formed the nucleus of a regular army. In 1885 the Ameer visited India in connection with the delimitation of his frontier on the side of Russia by means of a Joint Commission. Then occurred the collision between Afghans and Russians at Penjdeh which brought the two Empires to the verge of war. The danger was averted, and the Commission completed its labours, which were supplemented some years later by the delimitation of the frontier across the Pamirs. The immediate cause of the settlement in that elevated region, which is known figuratively as "the roof of the world," was the encroachment of Russian officers on Hunza-Nagar, two petty states dependent on Cashmere. The chiefs of these remote valleys were promised Russian protection and grew defiant. They thus brought down on themselves an Anglo-Indian expedition, and after some resolute opposition the valleys were occupied and, what is more important, the tribesmen, angry at their betrayal by Russia, have been quite won over to our side. Until this year the last incident in our frontier relations on the west was the Chitral campaign, when a small English force was besieged in the fort of that place, and rescued from its danger by a large expedition that advanced from the Peshawur Valley under General Sir Robert Low, and by a smaller force that marched across the glaciers and ice-bound paths from Gilgit under Colonel Kelly. A comparison between this campaign and that in Umbeyla thirty years before would show the immense progress made in the conduct of such enterprises by the improvement in weapons and organisation.

If the eastern frontier of India has never been so disturbed as the western, there have still been important events in that quarter. The Bhutan war in 1865, the Looshai expedition in the following year, and several minor contests with the Assamese tribes, exemplified the same lesson of the inevitable strife between a settled population and turbulent races that was apparent in the Punjab. But all these minor occurrences were overshadowed by the decision forced upon us in 1885 to bring the King of Burmah to his senses. In face of his insults and injuries we had been very long suffering, and no doubt we should under ordinary circumstances have put up with them still longer, but our action was hastened by the intentions of France, which contemplated a grand coup on the Irrawaddy. The invasion and easy conquest of Burmah was followed by its formal annexation, and in the 10 or 11 years that have since elapsed much has been done to develop its resources and to strengthen our position on the south-west frontier of China. It also brought us into contact with France on the Mekong, and as Lord Rosebery has stated a rupture was nearly caused between the two Powers by their antagonistic views as to the position of Siam. A termination was happily put to these threatening troubles by the Convention of January 1896 guaranteeing the independence and neutrality of Siam. Whatever changes may await our Indian Empire on both its frontiers diplomacy has done its best to define a clear and unmistakable position. We hold the promises of both Russia and France that they will not encroach on spheres of territory over which we claim not merely a prior but a superior interest.

But if the changes effected in India by war and policy have been great, those due to the introduction of railways and to the long period of internal peace which has allowed an extraordinary increase of both inhabitants and trade are certainly not inferior. The Queen's wars in the East have been wars it might almost be said for the preservation of peace. They have certainly kept strife and danger far removed from every home in India. When the Queen assumed personal responsibility the cost of administration rose by ten millions a year, and Indian financiers of the old school looked aghast as to where the money was to come from. The revenue of the Company never exceeded twenty-five millions sterling; that of the Queen has risen to over 92 millions in tens of rupees, bringing it down to about 53 millions sterling at the current rate of exchange. Of that revenue about ten millions is produced by the State railways, so that the Indian taxpayer after allowing for the increase in population pays considerably less than he did in 1857.

When the Mutiny broke out there was not a mile of railway, and all locomotion was carried on by dawk, the Indian diligence or stage coach, or by boat on the great rivers. It was by those means alone that troops could be moved to the front, and the long marches of our soldiers during that ordeal were not less remarkable than the extraordinary fighting powers they displayed. At the beginning of 1897 there were 21,000 miles of railway open for traffic, and another 1,000 miles in course of construction in India and Burmah. The majority of these lines had been built on definite and well-founded plans. There are the trunk lines connecting Bombay, the harbour nearest to Europe, with Calcutta and Madras, and both Bombay and Calcutta with Delhi, Lahore, and the Indus. Kurachee, the port of Scinde and in one sense of the whole of the western border, has been linked on to the Punjab, and will shortly be also connected with Bombay. Two lines have been carried across the Indus, one at Attock to Peshawur and the mouth of the Khyber Pass, the other across the Indus at Sukhur to Quettah and the Pisheen Valley with the mountain range forming its northern barrier tunnelled and everything in readiness to continue the railway to Candahar. In Burmah we have not been idle. Mandalay has been connected with Rangoon, the Mu Valley line is approaching the upper course of the Irrawaddy, and in a few months the Salween Valley will have been linked with our main system by the Kunlon Railway. Among the achievements of the Queen's rule in India railway construction must be allowed a foremost place, and there is no doubt that private enterprise will before very long give a fresh impetus to building new railways, especially in Burmah and Afghanistan.

If railways benefit the people by increasing trade and opening up the more inaccessible parts of the peninsula they also increase the security of the supreme Government, and in that way contribute to the credit of the country by inspiring confidence as to the stability of the existing order of things. Among their immediate advantages may also be classed the facilities they provide for the despatch of supplies to the districts affected by those terrible famines to which India has always been more or less subject, and with which owing to the generally increased density of the population it would without them be impossible to cope. But railways are in the first place and above all other considerations important because they aid the task of garrisoning India and indefinitely increase the mobile power of the executive. The estimate that would exclude them would certainly give a very partial and delusive idea of our position.

At the same time there has occurred a marked alteration in the military position in

India since the Mutiny. Before that event there were 25,000 European troops and 350,000 natives; now there are about 70,000 Europeans and 150,000 natives, and all the artillery except a few mountain batteries is European. It may fairly be said that in consequence of that rule we have not half enough artillery in India, but as one of security on paper the position may be pronounced perfect. The change is not one of mere numbers, it is also of composition. The native army of India is now composed of the pick of its fighting races, with a strong contingent of certainly not less than 10,000 men from those courageous and indomitable hillmen the Goorkhas of Nepaul. A sound policy, supplemented by the gracious demeanour and consideration of the Sovereign, has attracted to our side princes and races who looked askance at a mere mercantile Company, even when possessing great power, and who thought their dignity aspersed by subordination to it. The Princes have voluntarily made the arrangements which have resulted in the formation of the splendid Imperial Service Corps, the *élite* of the native states. This army already numbers 25,000 efficient troops and in course of time it will very likely reach twice that total. Its maintenance costs the Indian Exchequer practically nothing, and the most competent observers speak in the highest terms of its efficiency and military ardour. But important as is this addition to the fighting strength of India it is exceeded in importance by the almost unnoticed movement of the noble Rajput race—the only hereditary noble caste according to British ideas in India—towards our service. This tribute as to the respect in which our administration is held by certainly the most attractive race in India has come at the end of the Queen's era, and is of hopeful augury for the future. Without making any aspersion on the Company's Hindustani Sepoys, there is no room for doubt that the bulk of the present native army is composed of far superior material, and many different authorities agree in assigning a very high meed of excellence to the native Bengal and Punjab cavalry.

Reference has been made to the special interest taken by the Queen in her Eastern dependency. It was first shown in her Proclamation, and the tour made by the Prince of Wales in the cold season of 1875-6 throughout India was a further indication of that interest. The success of the tour, which gave actuality to the idea that India possessed a Sovereign, was immense, and from that time dates the desire of the most prominent native princes to visit the seat of Empire. Many have come, and others would have come but for difficulties of religious custom and civil etiquette which time alone can remove. During and after the Prince's visit the want was expressed for some title that should give the peoples of India a correct and suitable idea of their Sovereign's power and position, and in the course of 1876 it was announced that the Queen would add to her titles one more as the Empress of India. The announcement was received at home with some criticism, but the adoption of the Imperial style has exactly filled the void it was intended to occupy, and the princes and peoples of India accept it as the proper designation for the wielder of supreme power. In measuring the full effect of the transfer of power from the Company to the Queen it is desirable to recollect that the proclamation of Her Majesty as Empress of India on 1st January 1877 was the complement of the earlier proclamation in 1858.

Without asserting too positively that the present prosperous and peaceful condition of India represents the normal and permanent state of a country ruled under strange and it might almost be said impossible circumstances, there can be no hesitation in saying that the India of the Queen is more prosperous and contented than was the same State in the days of the East India Company. That Corporation ruled by fear alone, and even the trust in British good faith, complete as it was in a limited sense, never left the native rulers free from anxiety as to what might befall them after the temporary purposes of an engagement had been performed. This has now given place to a conviction that no ruler will be disturbed in his possessions except for gross misbehaviour, and that when removed those possessions will be transferred to his nearest or most suitable heir. The basis of the present harmony is mutual confidence, which the longer it endures must sink the deeper into the minds of both the rulers and the ruled in India. But this confidence has a still firmer root in the assumed and let it be said manifest power of the Sovereign and the British Government. In the last forty years many dangers have sprung up round India, and she has been drawn into the vortex of European politics. If the Company had survived till our time there can be no doubt that it would never have contemplated the possibility of accepting them with the serenity that the Imperial Government has displayed. It would certainly have resorted to that form of defence which is best carried out by offensive measures, and it would have gone forth with all its power to anticipate and dispel possible dangers in Central Asia and Indo-China. The Queen's Government, conscious of greater strength, has acted differently. It has seen the approach of Russia across the thousand miles of Central Asia without trepidation. The Company was disturbed when Russians were reported to be operating in Khiva, 1,500 miles from its frontier of that time: we are undisturbed when Russia's outposts are not a hundred miles from ours, and when we have drawn a line across the path of Russia from the Pamirs to Persia, the infraction of which we are bound to make a *casus belli.* There could not be more striking proof of the confidence of power than this. The situation is rendered the more dramatic and encouraging because that confidence is evidently shared by at least the militant Princes and races of India. Such a condition of things was impossible under the Company. It constitutes the reward of the personal efforts made by the Queen and her advisers to unify an Imperial India.